# Computational Models of Games

## ACM Distinguished Dissertations

**1982**

*Abstraction Mechanism and Language Design*
Paul N. Hilfinger

*Formal Specification of Interactive Graphics Programming Language*
William R. Mallgren

*Algorithmic Program Debugging*
Ehud Y. Shapiro

**1983**

*The Measurement of Visual Motion*
Ellen Catherine Hildreth

*Synthesis of Digital Designs from Recursion Equations*
Steven D. Johnson

**1984**

*Analytic Methods in the Analysis and Design of Number-Theoretic Algorithms*
Eric Bach

*Model-Based Image Matching Using Location*
Henry S. Baird

*A Geometric Investigation of Reach*
James U. Korein

**1985**

*Two Issues in Public-Key Cryptography*
Ben-Zion Chor

*The Connection Machine*
W. Daniel Hillis

**1986**

*All the Right Moves: A VLSI Architecture for Chess*
Carl Ebeling

*The Design and Evaluation of a High Performance Smalltalk System*
David Michael Ungar

**1987**

*Algorithm Animation*
Marc H. Brown

*The Rapid Evaluation of Potential Fields in Particle Systems*
Leslie Greengard

**1988**

*Computational Models of Games*
Anne Condon

*Trace Theory for Automatic Hierarchical Verification of Speed-Independent Circuits*
David L. Dill

# Computational Models of Games

Anne Condon

The MIT Press
Cambridge, Massachusetts
London, England

This book was printed and bound in the United States of America

Library of Congress Cataloging-in-Publication Data

Condon, Anne.
    Computational models of games / Anne Condon.
      p. cm. -- (ACM distinguished dissertations)
    ISBN 0-262-03152-3
    1. Game theory--Computer simulation. I. Title. II. Series.
  QA269.C596 1989
  519.3'01'13--dc20                     89-34498
                                            CIP

*To my parents*

*Robert and Mary*

# Contents

# List of Figures

# List of Tables

# Series Foreword

The doctoral thesis of Anne Condon, presented in this volume, was designated *Distinguished* by the selection committee for the 1988 Distinguished Doctoral Dissertation Award.

Sponsored by the Association for Computing Machinery and MIT Press, the Distinguished Doctoral Dissertation competition identifies the best doctoral theses in computer science and engineering submitted in the past year. The competition is extremely intense. More than 50 theses were nominated by universities from around the world. Dr. Condon's work emerged as an outstanding contribution of scientific research and scholarly writing.

Dr. Condon's thesis research, conducted under the direction of Professor Richard Ladner, provides a unified study of games. Games arise frequently in computer science in applications ranging from illustrating a complex problem solving domain in artificial intelligence (e.g. chess) to providing a model for adversarial relationships in cryptology. Condon's work unifies game concepts, such as Papadimitriou's games against nature and Babai's Arthur-Merlin games, with results from computational complexity theory, such as interactive proof systems and machine models including alternating Turing machines. New results then follow.

To accomplish this unification, Condon develops a new model of two person games called a *probabilistic game automaton*, abstracting characteristics of games such as secrecy, randomness and limitations on the power of the players. Complexity classes can then be defined enabling her to show, for example, that polynomial time games "against nature," that is, against an opponent making random moves, and games "against unknown nature," that is, against an opponent making random moves and having hidden information, accept the same class of languages as polynomial space bounded deterministic Turing machines.

Lawrence Snyder
Chair, ACM Distinguished Doctoral Dissertation Award
Selection Committee

# Preface

This book describes my thesis work on computational models of games. The thesis defines a general framework in which to model and understand computational problems that have game-like properties. Such problems arise in many diverse fields of Computer Science. Examples include the problem of computing optimal strategies for players in standard games and puzzles; problems involving the coordination of processors in a distributed system; cryptographic problems that arise in multi-party protocols; and optimization problems such as decision problems under uncertainty.

Randomness, secrecy and limited resources of the players are features that occur naturally in games, and these features also occur in the mathematical formulation of many of the above examples. Standard models of computation, such as Turing machines, do not provide a natural way to model these features. With the realization that game-like phenomena occur in computational problems, many researchers in Computer Science have developed models of computation that involve interaction between two or more players. These models provide a general framework in which the game-like properties of problems can be formulated. This framework can in turn be used to understand the complexity of game-like problems. Computational models of games that have motivated our research include the alternating Turing machines of Chandra, Kozen, and Stockmeyer, the games against nature of Papadimitriou, the Arthur-Merlin games of Babai, and the interactive proof systems of Goldwasser, Micali and Rackoff.

Our thesis extends earlier work on game-like models of computation. We define a new computational model of two person games, called a *probabilistic game automaton*. The model serves to unify the important features of previous models. We also prove a number of results on the complexity of several classes of problems encompassed by the probabilistic game automaton. These results help us understand how different features of game-like problems – randomness, secrecy and limited resources – influence their complexity. They address questions such as: Is it generally the case that secrecy makes it more difficult to compute an optimal strategy in a game? As an illustration, consider a typical card game such as bridge, which is a game of randomness (the cards are shuffled initially) and secrecy (players do not know what cards the other players have in their hands). Intuitively, we might expect that the secrecy makes it hard to devise a good strategy in bridge; if all the cards were face up – changing the game to one where there is no secrecy – it should be easier to decide on a good strategy.

To answer questions of this type, we define probabilistic game automata as language acceptors, where the input is accessible to both players and study the resulting complexity classes. Our results can be divided into two groups; those results on games in which the players are limited in the time they can use to compute their moves; and those in which they are limited in the space. Within these two groups, we compare games of bounded error, where the winner must win with high probability, with games of unbounded error, where the winner must win with probability at least 1/2. We also compare games of complete information, where both players can see all the moves of the game, with games of partial information, where players can make moves secretly. In addition to presenting our own results, we will systematically describe and relate similar results obtained by many other researchers.

Although our example of bridge helps to illustrate the nature of results, a more important measure of the value of such research is its application to problems of practical interest. We mention briefly here two nice examples; others are mentioned later in this book. One is the application of results on games against nature by Papadimitriou to pinpoint the complexity of optimization problems called decision problems under uncertainty; the other is the use of the notion of a zero knowledge interactive proof system, introduced by Goldwasser, Micali and Rackoff, in the design of secure cryptographic protocols. We believe that these game models are in some sense fundamental to the study of computational problems and expect that other applications will be found in the future.

Since the thesis was completed, some progress has been made in solving a number of open problems listed throughout this book. Also, different directions in the study of probabilistic game automata have been considered and some exciting new applications of these models have been discovered. For example, Dwork and Stockmeyer [13] did a thorough investigation of interactive proof systems with constant space bounded verifiers. New upper and lower bounds on the complexity of space bounded interactive proof systems were recently obtained by Lipton [26] and Condon and Lipton [10]. Applications of the proof techniques of all of these papers have yielded solutions to other open problems, including problems on the power of probabilistic finite state automata and on the rate of convergence of time-varying Markov chains. This demonstrates another reason to study computational models of games; they can provide a new way of thinking about and solving other problems. Unfortunately, these results are not presented here as this book is intended to reflect the work done in my thesis.

A different direction of research on computational models of games has been in the study of multi-person games. Results on these games can be found in Ben-or et al. [4], Fortnow et al. [15], Feige and Shamir [14] and Condon and Lipton [10]. Finally, Blum and Kannan [7] have applied ideas related to interactive proof systems to design a novel way of checking correctness of computer programs.

Anne Condon
University of Wisconsin-Madison
April, 1989

# Acknowledgements

I wish to thank my advisor, Richard Ladner, who collaborated with me on much of this research. He has provided much encouragement and support, and his insights throughout this research have been invaluable. It has been a real pleasure and privilege to work with him.

Thanks to Richard Anderson, Richard Ladner and Larry Ruzzo for their careful reading of a draft of this thesis. Their comments have led to many corrections and improvements to the presentation. In particular, Larry Ruzzo suggested a generalization to the model of a game automaton which is incorporated in this thesis. Also thanks to Faith Fich and Martin Tompa, who, in addition to those mentioned above, have contributed much to my education in general, through their excellent teaching, discussions and reviews of my work at every stage of the Ph. D. program.

Finally, thanks to everyone in the Computer Science Department at the University of Washington for providing an environment in which the pursuit of research has been an exceptionally enjoyable and rewarding experience. A special thanks to Heather Woll for sharing with me her enthusiasm for research and to Scott Rose for many valuable research discussions.

The research for this thesis was supported by the National Science Foundation under Grant number DCR-8402565, and by an IBM Graduate Fellowship.

# Computational Models of Games

# 1

# Introduction

Because games and game-like phenomena occur naturally in a computational setting, it is natural to formulate many problems in computer science in terms of games. For example, games like chess have been a challenge to researchers in artificial intelligence who desire models of thinking that can be automated. As a more recent example, researchers in distributed computing and cryptography have tried to develop models that reflect the competitive nature of distributed and cryptographic protocols.

In order to understand their complexity, various models of computation have been developed that reflect the game-like properties of these problems. This thesis presents a single computational model of games that unifies the important features of previous models. It is called the probabilistic game automaton. We show how it models in a natural way many problems that are of interest to computer scientists. We also relate the classes of problems encompassed by the model to standard complexity classes, thus providing insight into the complexity of the problems.

Before we describe the models that are the focus of this thesis, we illustrate some of the applications these models have in various fields of computer science. Some early applications were in understanding the complexity of logical theories [6] and in characterizing the complexity of games such as chess. Garey and Johnson [16], [22] list a number of games and puzzles whose complexity has been analyzed. These games include generalizations of chess and checkers as well as various pebble games and other games on graphs. More recently, games have been used to model cryptographic protocols that often involve interaction between two, possibly mistrustful, agents who wish to exchange information. A third 'player' in a cryptographic protocol is an eavesdropper, who tries to decrypt the conversation between the agents. Game-like models have been used to argue about the correctness and security of cryptographic protocols. For detailed examples of work that applies game-like models to cryptographic problems, see [19] or [8].

Game-theoretic ideas have been used in designing algorithms for distributed systems. In a distributed system, the processors need to compete for resources, but also need to co-operate in order that the system as a whole performs efficiently. The processors, or players, generally lack information on the complete state of the other processors in the system. Ben-Or and Linial applied the theory of voting schemes from game theory to develop algorithms for reaching agreement among processors of a distributed system [5]. Multi-person games offer the possibility of modeling distributed computation.

Finally, there are a number of examples where models of games have been used effectively in understanding problems that are of interest to computer scientists, but that do not superficially seem to have game-like qualities. One example of this is the work of Babai on the complexity of problems in group theory [2]. Babai showed that solutions to some computational problems in matrix groups such as membership and order could be verified with a high degree of confidence, using statistical evidence. Another example is the work of Papadimitriou [27] on the complexity of a class of problems in optimization — decision problems under uncertainty, that include variations of the job scheduling problem.

Traditional models of computation, such as Turing machines, do not reflect the game-like properties of many problems of interest to computer scientists. On the other hand, the traditional approach of mathematicians to game theory did not focus on questions regarding the computational complexity of a game. Many researchers in computer science have combined ideas from complexity theory and game theory to develop models of computation that involve interaction between two players [9], [28], [27], [2], [19].

We consider computational game models that consist of two competing players. The "board" of a computational game consists of an input, states and work tapes; and a step of a player consists of reading the tapes and changing the state. The difference between the traditional Turing model of computation and a computational game model is that in the Turing machine model, the steps, or transitions, of the machine are made by a single player, whereas in a computational game model the transitions are controlled by two competing players who have opposing goals. The goal of one player is to reach an accepting state and the goal of the other is to reach a rejecting state.

We describe three important features of games, each of which is included in some subset of the computational game models already studied.

- *Randomness.* Each player can make random choices, such as shuffling a deck of cards, rolling dice or flipping a coin.

- *Secrecy.* Each player can keep information about its moves private from the other player. A game such as chess, where both players can see all the moves of the game, is called a game of complete information whereas a game such as bridge, where players keep information secret, is called a game of partial information.

- *Limited resources.* Each player may have a limited amount of computational resources in which to carry out its strategy.

Randomness is modeled using coin tossing in a way similar to the way it is modeled in the probabilistic Turing machines of Gill [17]. Secrecy is modeled in a way similar to the way it is modeled in the private alternating Turing machines of Peterson and Reif [28], by allowing each player to have private work tapes and states that are not visible to its opponent. Limited resources are modeled by standard time and space bounds and by whether or not non-deterministic choice is allowed.

In order to say what it means for a computational game to solve a problem, and in order to compare these games with standard models of computation, the games are defined to be language acceptors. The players share an input, which determines the initial configuration of the game. An input is accepted by a game if a designated player has a winning strategy on that input. To make clearer how a game can be thought of as a language acceptor, consider a computational game that receives as input a positive integer $N$, which represents the length of a generalized checkers board, and a position $(i, j)$ for each piece on the board, where $1 \leq i, j \leq N$. Suppose the computational game is defined so that one player simulates the player moving the black pieces and the other player simulates the player moving the white pieces. An input is accepted if the player moving the black pieces can force a win in the game, starting from the positions given in the input. Thus the language recognized by the computational game is the set of all configurations of an $N \times N$ checkers game where blacks can force a win, for all $N$.

## 1.1    Previous Work

Over the last decade, a number of models of computational games have been introduced and their associated complexity classes analyzed. We outline some of these models here. In Chapter 2 we will define them more precisely and give concrete examples of problems they model. The best known game-theoretic model of computation is probably the *alternating Turing machine* [9], that models a two-person game where both players can make nondeterministic moves. Neither player tosses coins and both players have complete information of all the moves of the game. The machine accepts an input if one player, designated at the outset of the game, has a winning strategy, defined here to be a strategy that forces the machine to go into an accepting state regardless of what strategy the other player employs. Alternating Turing machines model games such as $N \times N$ checkers or Generalized Geography (see [16] for descriptions of these games) and also model some logical theories [6]. Reif [30] has extended the definition of alternating Turing machines to two-person games with no randomness, where the players hide moves from each other. Peterson and Reif have considered multi-person games [28]. A special class of games, called *solitaire games*, where one player must play deterministically after its first move, has been studied by Ladner and Norman [25].

The *games against nature* of Papadimitriou [27] are another example of two-person games of complete information - that is, both players can see all the moves of the game. An interesting feature of games against nature not shared by the models of the last paragraph is that one player, simulating nature, plays randomly. The other player, who can move nondeterministically, chooses a strategy that maximizes its probability of winning against the random player. A strategy of this player that leads to a win with probability $> \frac{1}{2}$ against the random player is considered to be a winning strategy. An input on which the nondeterministic player has a winning strategy is considered to be *accepted* by the game. The randomness in games against nature provides a natural way to model a branch of problems in optimization: decision problems under uncertainty. We will describe one example of such a problem in Chapter 3.

Decision problems under uncertainty are examples of problems in which randomness is used in the problem definition. Other, quite different research, has shown that randomness is a useful resource in solving computational problems whose definition does not include randomness. Probably the best-known example of this is the primality testing algorithm of Rabin [29]. As a result, there has been much interest in complexity classes that extend deterministic classes by the addition of randomness. Examples are the classes $RP$ [17], which extends the class $P$ of languages that have deterministic polynomial time algorithms, or $RNC$, which generalizes in a similar way the class $NC$ of languages that can be recognized by uniform families of circuits with polynomial size and polylog depth [11]. Two models of games were introduced independently in 1985 that carry the idea of extending a computational model by adding randomness a step further. One is the *Arthur-Merlin games* of Babai [2]; the other the *interactive proof systems* of Goldwasser, Micali and Rackoff [19]. Both of these models extend nondeterministic Turing machines by adding randomness in different ways.

Motivating these models is the notion that the class $NP$ consists of those languages that have efficient "proofs of membership". That is, a prover can convince a deterministic polynomial time verifier that a string is in an $NP$ language by presenting a witness of that fact to the verifier. Suppose that the power of the verifier is extended so that it can flip coins and can interact with the prover during the course of a proof. In this way, the verifier can gather statistical evidence that an input is in a language, instead of just receiving a witness. An intriguing question is whether this extends the class of languages that have efficient proofs of membership.

Interactive proof systems and Arthur-Merlin games provide two ways of formalizing this question. In an Arthur-Merlin game, Merlin wishes to prove membership of the input in some language to Arthur; Arthur can toss coins and accepts statistical evidence as proof. If Merlin can convince Arthur with high probability, then the input is accepted. The difference between Arthur-Merlin games and games against nature is that, in a game against nature, the nondeterministic player need only win with probability $> \frac{1}{2}$ against the random player in order for an input to be accepted, whereas in an Arthur-Merlin game the non-random player must win with probability bounded away from $\frac{1}{2}$ by a constant for an input to be accepted. Interactive proof systems are similar to Arthur-Merlin games. However, the random player, called the verifier, can keep some information about its moves private from the other player, called the prover. Later in Chapter 2 we will present an interesting example of a language which is not known to be in *NP* but has an efficient interactive proof.

# 1.2    Contributions of this Thesis

The goals of this thesis are two-fold; first to define a computational model of games that unifies and extends the models discussed in the last section; and second, to investigate the complexity of the resulting model. We summarize our progress in achieving these goals in this section.

## 1.2.1    Definition of a Probabilistic Game Automaton

We introduce a new model of computational games, called a probabilistic game automaton. We give a detailed description of a probabilistic game automaton in Chapter 2. It includes the three important features of the games described above — randomness, secrecy and limited resources. Each of the models mentioned in Section 1.1 are encompassed by our model. The model also includes new models of games, such as *games against unknown nature*, a class of games similar to games against nature except that the nondeterministic player does not see all the moves of the random player, or nature.

The players of a probabilistic game automaton are named player 0 and player 1. Each player can take *coin-tossing* steps where the player flips a coin to determine its next step. On other steps, the player can choose which step to take from the possible next steps. A step of player 1 made by choice, rather than by flipping a coin, is called an *existential* step. Similarly, a step of player 0 that is not coin-tossing is called a *universal* step. We use these names to distinguish steps where a player has a choice from the coin-tossing steps. The names are derived from the fact that we are interested in whether there *exists* a strategy of player 1 such that *for all* strategies of player 0, player 1 wins the game with high probability. Thus a game consists of a sequence of existential, universal and coin-tossing steps, in any order.

To investigate the complexity of different types of probabilistic game automata we define the automata as language acceptors. The notion of acceptance of an input is defined in terms of strategies of player 1. A strategy of player 1 is a winning strategy with bound $\epsilon \geq 0$ if the probability that the strategy leads to a win for player 1 is $> \frac{1}{2} + \epsilon$ and is a losing strategy with bound $\epsilon \geq 0$ if the probability that the strategy leads to a win for player 1 is $\leq \frac{1}{2} - \epsilon$. A probabilistic game automaton is *bounded random* if there is an $\epsilon > 0$ such that for each input there is either a winning strategy for player 1 with bound $\epsilon$ or every strategy is a losing strategy with bound $\epsilon$. A probabilistic game automaton is *unbounded random* if for each input there is a winning strategy for player 1 with bound 0 or every strategy is a losing strategy with bound 0. The language accepted by a bounded (unbounded) random game automaton is the set of inputs for which player 1 has a winning strategy with bound $\epsilon > 0$ ($\epsilon = 0$).

Each player displays various *degrees of information* to the other player. To model this, we assign private work tapes and visible work tapes to the players on which to record their moves. The moves of a player can depend on the contents of its private work tapes and on the visible work tapes of both itself and the other player. If a player never uses its private work tapes then we say that the player displays *complete information*. If a player uses only its private work tapes then the player reveals no information to its opponent and we say that the player displays *zero information*. In general, a player displays *partial information* as it uses both private and visible work tapes.

Throughout this thesis we make the assumption that player 1 displays complete information. We study this restricted model because it is simpler, and yet it is general enough to encompass all of the models already studied in the literature. The results of the thesis do not necessarily extend to the more general model where player 1 displays partial information, and we recommend that the more general model be studied in the future. Based on our assumption that player 1 displays complete information, we can make a simplification to our model without loss of generality, namely that all the coin-tossing steps are made by player 0. Intuitively this simplification does not weaken the model because player 0 can toss all the coins needed by player 1 in a game. This is further explained in Chapter 2.

The model includes many different types of game automaton, where player 0 is restricted in some way. We introduce a notation to specify the various types of probabilistic game automata. The symbol $\forall$ is used to denote that player 0 can take universal steps. If $M$ is an unbounded random game automaton, then the letter $U$ is used to denote that player 0 can take coin-tossing steps; if $M$ is a bounded random game automaton then the letter $B$ is used. Finally the letters $Z$, $P$ or $C$ are used to denote that player 0 displays zero, partial or complete information, respectively. Table 1.1 summarizes this notation.

| Universal steps | Coin-tossing steps | Degree of information |
|---|---|---|
| $\forall$ | $U$ (bounded) | $Z$ (zero) |
| | $B$ (unbounded) | $P$ (partial) |
| | | $C$ (complete) |

Table 1.1: *Notation used to specify types of probabilistic game automata.*

To specify the restrictions on player 0, at most one symbol is taken from each of the left two columns and exactly one from the third column. For example, $UC$ refers to the class of unbounded game automata where player 0 displays complete information and does not take universal steps. $\forall C$ refers to the class of game automata where there are no coin-tossing steps, player 0 can take universal steps and displays complete information; more simply stated, $\forall C$ refers to alternating Turing machines. Probabilistic game automata can be time bounded or space bounded. For example, $UC\text{–}TIME(t(n))$ is the class of languages accepted by $UC$ game automata that run in time bounded by $O(t(n))$. Similarly, $UP\text{–}SPACE(s(n))$ is the class of languages accepted by $UP$ game automata that run in space bounded by $O(s(n))$.

To conclude Chapter 2, we present some fundamental results on probabilistic game automata. We show that the probabilistic game automaton is a reasonable model of computation in that it accepts exactly the recursively enumerable sets. Secondly, we show that in a game with complete information, if player 1 has a winning strategy then it has one that depends only on the current configuration visible to player 1, and not on the whole history of the game. This result simplifies the analysis of games with complete information in later chapters.

## 1.2.2   New Results on the Complexity of Probabilistic Game Automata

The remainder of the thesis is a study of the complexity of different models encompassed by the probabilistic game automaton. One motivation for this is to understand the effect of varying the parameters of randomness, secrecy and limited resources, which are the three features of games included in our model. Another is that by relating computational game models to standard complexity classes, the complexity of those problems naturally modeled by the game models can be better understood. We summarize previous work on complexity of game models and prove new results. These results, which we briefly discuss in the remainder of this chapter, are presented in Chapters 3, 4 and 5.

### Time Bounded Game Automata

In Chapter 3, results on time bounded game automata are presented. There has been much interest in polynomial time bounded games against nature, Arthur-Merlin games and interactive proof systems. Papadimitriou [27] compared games against nature, which are unbounded random game automata with complete information, and alternating Turing machines, which are game automata with complete information and no randomness. He showed that polynomial time games against nature and alternating Turing machines accept the same class of languages. Also, Chandra, Kozen and Stockmeyer [9] showed that polynomial time alternating Turing machines accept the same class of languages as polynomial space deterministic Turing machines. In our notation, these results are

$$UC\text{--}TIME(poly(n)) = \forall C\text{--}TIME(poly(n)) = PSPACE \ .$$

We generalize Papadimitriou's result to the class of probabilistic game automata $UP$, which we call *games against unknown nature*. This class consists of game automata with both partial information and randomness, where player 0 makes no universal steps. We show that any language accepted by a game automaton in the class $UP$, which is $t(n)$ time bounded, is also accepted by an alternating Turing machine which is $t^2(n)$ time bounded. Thus partial information does not increase the complexity of games against nature significantly.

The following two formulas summarize our results on unbounded random game automata. For time constructible $t(n)$,

$$\forall C\text{–}TIME(t(n)) \subseteq \forall UC\text{–}TIME(t(n)) \subseteq \forall C\text{–}TIME(t(n)\log t(n)) \text{ and}$$

$$UC\text{–}TIME(t(n)) \subseteq UP\text{–}TIME(t(n)) \subseteq UC\text{–}TIME(t^2(n)) .$$

Using quite different techniques, an analogous result for bounded random game automata was proved by Goldwasser and Sipser [20]. They showed that polynomial time bounded interactive proof systems and Arthur-Merlin games accept the same class of languages, that is,

$$BP\text{–}TIME(poly(n)) = BC\text{–}TIME(poly(n)) .$$

In Table 1.2, we summarize some of the known results on polynomial time bounded game automata. The table characterizes Arthur-Merlin games, interactive proof systems, games against nature, games against unknown nature and alternating Turing machines. Later we present a similar table for space bounded game automata, so that the results for time and space bounded game automata can be compared easily.

$$
\begin{array}{ccccc}
BP\text{–}TIME(poly(n)) & \subseteq & UP\text{–}TIME(poly(n)) & = & \forall P\text{–}TIME(poly(n)) \\
\shortparallel & & \shortparallel & & \shortparallel \\
BC\text{–}TIME(poly(n)) & \subseteq & UC\text{–}TIME(poly(n)) & = & \forall C\text{–}TIME(poly(n)) \\
\cup | & & & & \shortparallel \\
NP & & & & PSPACE
\end{array}
$$

Table 1.2: *Summary of results on time bounded game automata.*

## Space Bounded Game Automata with Complete Information

Unlike time bounded game automata, not much work has previously been done on space bounded game automata. In Chapter 4, we consider space bounded game automata with complete information. We characterize the space bounded analogues of games against nature and Arthur-Merlin games.

In our notation, the classes of languages accepted by these game automata with space bound $s(n)$ are $UC\text{--}SPACE(s(n))$ and $BC\text{--}SPACE(s(n))$, respectively. Our main result is that for space constructible $s(n) = \Omega(\log n)$,

$$BC\text{--}SPACE(s(n)) = UC\text{--}SPACE(s(n)) = \forall C\text{--}SPACE(s(n)) .$$

Chandra, Kozen and Stockmeyer [9] showed that for $s(n) = \Omega(\log n)$,

$$\forall C\text{--}SPACE(s(n)) \subseteq \cup_{c \geq 0} DTIME(2^{cs(n)}) .$$

As a special case of these results, logarithmic space bounded Arthur-Merlin games and games against nature accept the same class of languages as deterministic polynomial time bounded deterministic Turing machines. Thus

$$BC\text{--}SPACE(\log n) = UC\text{--}SPACE(\log n) = P .$$

In contrast, recall that in the case of polynomial time bounded games, the class of languages accepted by Arthur-Merlin games is not known to be equal to the class of languages accepted by games against nature. In fact this is the first instance known to us of the equivalence of two complexity classes that differ only in that one is unbounded random and the other is bounded random. The fact that $UC\text{--}SPACE(\log n) = P$ parallels Papadimitriou's result for time bounded game automata that $UC\text{--}TIME(poly(n)) = PSPACE$. The proof of the result for space bounded games against nature is based on the fact that such games can be modeled as Markov decision processes, which are a generalization of Markov processes [12]. Markov decision processes have been used to model many problems in optimization and control; they are described in Chapter 4 together with their relationship to space bounded games against nature.

The above results characterize logarithmic space bounded games against nature and Arthur-Merlin games. However they do not extend to game automata with universal steps, that is, logarithmic space bounded game automata in the classes $\forall UC$ and $\forall BC$. The best results we can prove on these classes are:

$$P \subseteq \forall BC\text{--}SPACE(\log n) \subseteq \forall UC\text{--}SPACE(\log n) \subseteq NP .$$

## Space Bounded Game Automata with Partial Information

We compare space bounded game automata with partial information to those with complete information in Chapter 5. We show that partial information adds complexity to space bounded game automata. In particular we show that for space constructible $s(n) = \Omega(n)$,

$$BC\text{--}SPACE(s(n)) \subseteq BP\text{--}SPACE(\log s(n)) \text{ and}$$

$$UC\text{--}SPACE(s(n)) \subseteq UP\text{--}SPACE(\log s(n)) \, .$$

Combining these results with the results of Chapter 4, it follows that any language in deterministic exponential time can be recognized in logarithmic space by a game automaton in the class $BP$. Using the analogy of these game automata with interactive proof systems, we can say that if $L$ is any language in deterministic exponential time, then membership in $L$ can be proved interactively in logarithmic space. Thus, $DTIME(2^{poly(n)}) \subseteq BP\text{--}SPACE(\log n)$. Table 1.3 summarizes these results on space bounded probabilistic game automata.

$$
\begin{array}{ccccc}
BP\text{--}SPACE(\log n) & \subseteq & UP\text{--}SPACE(\log n) & \supseteq & \forall P\text{--}SPACE(\log n) \\
\cup| & & \cup| & & || \\
BC\text{--}SPACE(poly(n)) & = & UC\text{--}SPACE(poly(n)) & = & \forall C\text{--}SPACE(poly(n)) \\
\cup| & & & & || \\
PSPACE & & & & \cup_{c \geq 0} DTIME(2^{n^c})
\end{array}
$$

Table 1.3: *Summary of results on space bounded game automata.*

We do not have a complete characterization of space bounded game automata with partial information in terms of standard complexity classes. We cannot show, for example, that logarithmic space interactive proof systems accept the same class of languages as polynomial space Arthur-Merlin games. We discuss in Chapter 5 why these classes are hard to analyze. We also present there some results that characterize space bounded game automata when the strategies of the players are history bounded. Informally, a game automaton is $h(n)$ history bounded if on inputs $x$ of length $n$ that are accepted by $M$, player 1 has a winning strategy on $x$ with the following property. The value of the strategy on any history visible to player 1 depends only on the last $h(n)$ configurations of the history visible to player 1.

We consider game automata with simultaneous space and history bounds. For example, $UP\text{–}SPACE, HIS(s(n), h(n))$ denotes the class of unbounded random game automata that have simultaneous space bound $s(n)$ and history bound $h(n)$. Game automata with history bound 1 are called Markov game automata. This is a natural class of game automata to consider, since it restricts the strategy of player 1 to depend only on the current configuration visible to it, and not on the previous history of the game. We show that $s(n)$ space bounded Markov game automata recognize the same class of languages as nondeterministic Turing machines which have time bound exponential in $s(n)$. For example, $UP\text{–}SPACE, HIS(\log n, 1) = NTIME(poly(n))$. In the more general case, we show that the history bound of a game can be decreased at the cost of increasing the space. If $h(n)$ is space constructible then

$$UP\text{–}SPACE, HIS(s(n), h(n)) \subseteq UP\text{–}SPACE, HIS(s(n) + h(n), O(1)) \ .$$

The conclusions of the thesis and open problems are described in Chapter 6.

# 2

## Probabilistic Game Automata

We describe here our model of a computational game, called a probabilistic game automaton. Before getting to the formal definition, we list informally the main components of a probabilistic game automaton, $M$ with two players, player 0 and player 1. Figure 2.1 shows a probabilistic game automaton with two visible worktapes and one private worktape for each player. Assume that $M$ has an input alphabet and a worktape alphabet and $k$ tapes. The $k$ tapes of $M$ plus the input tape are divided into three disjoint groups: the *visible tapes* and the *tapes private* to player $i, i = 0, 1$. The input tape is one of the visible tapes and is read-only. Each player has a *private head* on each of its private tapes and all of the visible tapes. The private head on a visible tape allows the player to read, undetected by the other player, what is written on the visible tape. In addition each player has a *visible head* on each visible tape. All the tapes are one-way infinite.

There is a special bit called a *turn indicator* that has the value $i$ when the next step of $M$ is made by player $i$. The states of $M$ are triples from some finite set $V \times P_0 \times P_1$, where $V$ is a set of visible substates and $P_i$ is a set of substates private to player $i, i = 0, 1$. Each set $V, P_0$ and $P_1$ contains a coin-tossing substate, denoted by $vc, p_0c$ and $p_1c$, respectively. A state $(v, p_0, p_1)$ is called a *coin-tossing* state if $v = vc$ or if the value of the turn indicator is $i$ and $p_i = p_ic$. Some subset of the states of $M$ is called the set of *halting* states, which itself is partitioned into *accepting* and *rejecting* states.

There is a *transition function* $\delta_i$ for each player that defines the valid steps of player $i$ of $M$. At any moment, player $i$ has exactly two valid steps. If the player wishes to move deterministically then the two steps are the same. In a

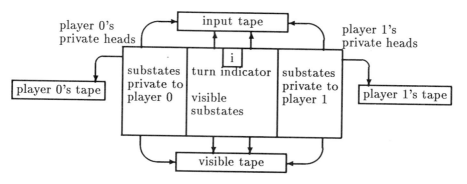

Figure 2.1: *A probabilistic game automaton with two visible tapes and one private tape for each player.*

step, player $i$ may change the visible substate, player $i$'s private substate, the contents of the tapes under the visible heads and under the private heads of player $i$. Also player $i$ may shift these heads one tape cell to the right or left and may change the turn indicator so that player $1 - i$ moves at the next step.

## 2.1 Definition of a Probabilistic Game Automaton

We now give a formal definition of a probabilistic game automaton. To help understand the definitions, the formalisms are motivated intuitively and a simple example of a probabilistic game automaton is used to illustrate the definitions. In Section 2.2, a notation is described that is used throughout the thesis to classify in a uniform way the different game models encompassed by our general definition. Interesting examples of computational game models are given in Section 2.3. The chapter closes in Section 2.4 with two theorems that prove general properties of probabilistic game automata.

A $k$-tape probabilistic game automaton with two players: player 0, which has $p_0$ private tapes and player 1, which has $p_1$ private tapes, is a Turing machine of the form

$$M = (V, P_0, P_1, \Sigma, \Gamma, \delta_0, \delta_1, F, A, s, \not{b}, vc, p_0c, p_1c),$$

where
> $V$ is a finite set of visible substates,
> $P_i$ is the finite set of private substates of player $i, i = 0, 1$,
> $\Sigma$ is a finite input alphabet, $\Sigma \subseteq \Gamma$,
> $\Gamma$ is a finite tape alphabet,
> $F$ is the set of halting substates, $F \subseteq V$,
> $A \subseteq F$ is the set of accepting substates,
> $F - A$ is the set of rejecting substates,
> $s$ is the start state, $s \in V \times P_0 \times P_1$,
> $\not{b}$ is the blank symbol, $\not{b} \in \Gamma - \Sigma$,
> $vc$ is the visible coin-tossing substate, $vc \in V$,
> $p_i c$ is player $i$'s private coin-tossing substate, $p_i c \in P_i, i = 0, 1$,
> $\delta_i$ is the transition relation for player $i$, defined by
> $$\delta_i : (V - F) \times P_i \times \Gamma^{3k+3-2p_i-3p_{1-i}}$$
> $$\rightarrow (V \times P_i \times \{0, 1\} \times (\Gamma - \{\not{b}\})^{2k-p_i-2p_{1-i}} \times \{R, L, S\}^{2k+2-p_i-2p_{1-i}})^2.$$

The domain of the transition relation for player $i$ contains the visible substate, the private substate of player $i$ and the contents of the tape cells that are pointed to by heads visible to player $i$. The transition relation is not defined when the visible substate is a final substate. There are $k$ tapes plus an input tape; hence there are $k + 1 - (p_0 + p_1)$ tapes that are not private to any player. Each of these tapes has four heads, one private head and one visible head for each player. Three of these heads are visible to player $i$. Also each of the $p_i$ private tapes has one head visible to player $i$. Thus there are $3k+3-2p_i-3p_{1-i}$ tape cells visible to player $i$ when it takes a step; hence the term $\Gamma^{3k+3-2p_i-3p_{1-i}}$ in the domain of $\delta_i$. There are two possible steps for player $i$; hence the range of $\delta_i$ is a pair of tuples, each of whose components list all the changes made to the states, worktapes and heads of the game at a step. In a step, player $i$ may change the visible state, private substate of player $i$ and the turn indicator. Player $i$ may change the contents of any of the worktape cells that are pointed to by one of player $i$'s tape heads, and may move any of its heads left or right, or not move it at all. Player $i$ has $2k - p_i - 2p_{1-i}$ worktape heads and 2 input heads.

We make a distinction between a *step* and a *move*. A move by player $i$ is a sequence of steps, or transitions, that begins just after the turn indicator is first set to $i$ and ends when the turn indicator is set to $1 - i$.

### 2.1.1 Configurations and Histories

Now that we have given the definition of a probabilistic game automaton, we need to introduce some notation in order to be able to describe formally what is meant by a strategy and acceptance of an input. We build up to this in the next few sections, starting with configurations and histories.

A *configuration* of $M$ on input $x$ is a tuple $C$, whose components are the current state of $M$, the turn indicator, the current positions of the heads on the tapes of $M$ and the tape contents. Formally, a configuration $C$ of $M$ on input $x$ is a $(5k - 3p_0 - 3p_1 + 9)$-tuple

$$
\begin{aligned}
C = (&v, p_0, p_1, t, ph_0^0, \ldots, ph_{k-p_1}^0, vh_0^0, \ldots, vh_{k-p_0-p_1}^0, ph_0^1, \ldots, ph_{k-p_0}^1, \\
&vh_0^1, \ldots, vh_{k-p_0-p_1}^1, \alpha_1^0, \ldots, \alpha_{p_0}^0, \alpha_1^1, \ldots, \alpha_{p_1}^1, \alpha_0^v, \ldots, \alpha_{k-p_0-p_1}^v).
\end{aligned}
$$

Here $(v, p_0, p_1)$ is the state of $M$ and $t \in \{0, 1\}$ is the value of the turn indicator. The numbers $ph_0^i, \ldots ph_{k-p_{1-i}}^i$ are the positions of the private heads of player $i$ and the numbers $vh_0^i, \ldots, vh_{k-p_0-p_1}^i$ are the positions of the visible heads of player $i$. The head positions are positive integers, with position 1 being the leftmost tape position of a tape. Each $\alpha_i$ is a string in $\Gamma^*$ representing the contents of tape $i$. $\alpha_0^v$ is the input $x$.

We define $visible(C, i)$ to be a tuple whose components are the part of configuration $C$ that is visible to player $i$. This consists of the components of $C$, less the contents of the private tapes of player $1 - i$, the private head positions of player $1 - i$, and the substate of player $1 - i$. Thus

$$
\begin{aligned}
visible(C, i) = (&v, p_i, t, ph_0^i, \ldots, ph_{k-p_{1-i}}^i, vh_0^i, \ldots, vh_{k-p_i-p_{1-i}}^i, \\
&vh_0^{1-i}, \ldots, vh_{k-p_i-p_{1-i}}^{1-i}, \alpha_1^i, \ldots, \alpha_{p_i}^i, \alpha_0^v, \ldots, \alpha_{k-p_0-p_1}^v).
\end{aligned}
$$

Similarly let $invisible(C, i)$ be the part of configuration $C$ that is not visible to player $i$, that is,

$$
invisible(C, i) = (p_{1-i}, ph_0^{1-i}, \ldots, ph_{k-p_i}^{1-i}, \alpha_1^{1-i}, \ldots, \alpha_{p_{1-i}}^{1-i}).
$$

Finally, $visible(C)$ is the part of configuration $C$ that is visible to both players:

$$
visible(C) = (v, t, vh_0^0, \ldots, vh_{k-p_0-p_1}^0, vh_0^1, \ldots, vh_{k-p_0-p_1}^1, \alpha_0^v, \ldots, \alpha_{k-p_0-p_1}^v).
$$

Associated with the transition functions $\delta_i$ is a *step relation*, $\rightarrow$, that maps configurations to configurations in the usual way for a Turing machine.

Let $player(C)$ be the value of the turn indicator of configuration $C$, $state(C)$ be the state of $C$, which is a triple $(v, p_0, p_1)$, and let $init(M, x)$ be the initial configuration of $M$ on input $x$. If player 0 makes the first move of $M$, then

$$init(M, x) = (s, 0, 1, \ldots, 1, \lambda, \ldots, \lambda, x, \lambda, \ldots, \lambda) \, ,$$

where $\lambda$ denotes the empty string. The configurations are partitioned into a few different types. If $state(C)$ is coin-tossing, that is, if $v = vc$ or if $player(C) = i$ and $p_i = p_ic$, we say $C$ is coin-tossing ($\mathcal{R}$). Similarly if $C$ is accepting, that is, $v \in A$, the set of accepting substates, or rejecting, that is, $v \in F - A$, the set of rejecting substates, we say $C$ is accepting ($a$) or rejecting ($r$), respectively. Otherwise if $player(C) = 0$ we say $C$ is universal ($\forall$) and if $player(C) = 1$ we say $C$ is existential ($\exists$). We say that player 0 takes a universal step if player 0 takes a step from a universal configuration. We define an existential step of player 1 similarly. We call a step that is neither universal or existential a coin-tossing step.

A *history* $H$ for $M$ on input $x$ is a sequence $C_0 C_1 \ldots C_n$ such that $C_j \rightarrow C_{j+1}$ for $0 \leq j \leq n-1$ and $C_0 = init(M, x)$. Intuitively, a history records a sequence of steps of a game. We define $last(H)$ to be $C_n$ and we say that $H$ has length $n$. Let $visible(H, i)$ be the part of the history visible to player $i$. Formally, if $H$ is a configuration, $visible(H, i)$ is already defined. Otherwise let $HD$ be a history where $H$ itself is a history. Then

$$visible(HD, i) = \begin{cases} visible(H, i), \text{if } visible(last(H), i) = visible(D, i), \\ visible(H, i)visible(D, i), \text{otherwise}. \end{cases}$$

Intuitively, $visible(H, i)$ records all the changes to the tapes and states visible to player $i$ during history $H$. For example, if player $1 - i$ writes to a certain visible tape cell and then rewrites to the same cell during a move, both symbols written to that cell are recorded in the visible history of player $i$, even though by the time the turn indicator changes to $i$, the first symbol is no longer visible to player $i$. An alternative way to define the visible history of player $i$ would be as the sequence of configurations visible to player $i$ when the turn indicator is $i$. In this case, if player $1 - i$ writes to a certain visible tape cell and then rewrites to the same cell during a move, player $i$ would only see the second symbol written to the visible tape cell, and not the first. For the results about probabilistic game automata in this thesis, both definitions are equivalent. We shall always assume the former definition throughout the thesis. In general one player will not know how many steps the other player is taking during the other player's move. This enables a player to do a lot of work privately without the other player knowing anything about how much work has been done.

Finally let $visible(H)$ be the part of the history $H$ visible to both players. A history $H$ is called a *full history* if $state(last(H))$ is halting.

**Example 2.1** *A simple probabilistic game automaton.*

We give a simple example of a probabilistic game automaton, which illustrates the above definitions. More interesting examples of probabilistic game automata will be described in Section 2.3. Consider a game where player 0 tosses two coins in private; then player 1 guesses the two coin tosses of player 0. If player 1 guesses the coin tosses correctly, the accepting state is entered; otherwise the rejecting state is entered. We describe a probabilistic game automaton $M$ that simulates this game. We first list the states of $M$. The private substates of player 0 are $\{init\} \cup \{a, ab \mid a, b \in \{h, t\}\}$. $init$ is the initial private substate and $h, t$ represent heads and tails, respectively. The set of visible substates is $\{init\} \cup \{a, ab \mid a, b \in \{h, t\}\} \cup \{accept, reject\}$. Player 1 has no private substates. The game automaton $M$ has no worktapes and does not read its input; hence for simplicity we represent a configuration as a 3-tuple:

$$(visible\ substate,\ private\ substate\ of\ player\ 0,\ turn\ indicator).$$

The initial configuration is $(init, init, 0)$. A configuration visible to player 1 is a pair $(visible\ substate,\ turn\ indicator)$. The step relation between the configurations is given in Table 2.1.

An example of a history $H$ of $M$ is

$$(init, init, 0)\ (init, h, 0)\ (init, ht, 1)\ (h, ht, 1)\ (hh, ht, 0)\ (reject, ht, 0)\ .$$

The history records a game where player 0 tosses heads, then tails, in private and player 1 guesses that player 0 tossed two heads. Note that $visible(H, 1)$ is

$$(init, 0)\ (init, 1)\ (h, 1)\ (hh, 0)\ (reject, 0)\ .$$

| Configuration $C$ | $\{C' \mid C \to C'\}$ |
|:---:|:---:|
| $(init, init, 0)$ | $\{(init, a, 0) \mid a \in \{h, t\} \}$ |
| $(init, a, 0), \quad a \in \{h, t\}$ | $\{(init, ab, 1) \mid b \in \{h, t\}\}$ |
| $(init, ab, 1), \quad a, b \in \{h, t\}$ | $\{(c, ab, 1) \mid c \in \{h, t\} \}$ |
| $(c, ab, 1), \quad a, b, c \in \{h, t\}$ | $\{(cd, ab, 0) \mid d \in \{h, t\} \}$ |
| $(ab, ab, 0), \quad a, b \in \{h, t\}$ | $\{(accept, ab, 0)\}$ |
| $(cd, ab, 0), \quad a, b, c, d \in \{h, t\}$ | $\{(reject, ab, 0)\}$ |
| $a \neq b$ or $c \neq d$ | |

Table 2.1: *Definition of the step relation ($\to$) of the probabilistic game automaton $M$, Example 2.1.*

### 2.1.2   Degree of Information

Player 0 may display varying *degrees of information* to player 1. If player 0 never changes its visible substate and never moves its visible tape heads, we say player 0 displays *zero* information. In such a game, the only action of player 0 which is visible to player 1 is that player 0 changes the turn indicator. If player 0 never changes its private substate and never reads or writes on its private tapes, we say player 0 displays *complete* information. In general player 0 displays *partial* information. A game where player 0 displays complete or zero information is a special case of a game where player 0 displays partial information.

### 2.1.3   Strategies

Since a player does not have access to the private tapes and substates the other player, its steps can only depend on what it has seen so far in the game. To make this precise we define a *strategy* of player 1 of $M$ on input $x$ to be a function $\sigma$ mapping histories visible to player 1 on input $x$ into configurations visible to player 1 with the property that if $H$ is a history such that $last(H)$ is not a coin-tossing configuration and $player(H) = 1$ then then $HC$ is a history where $C$ is a configuration such that $\sigma(visible(H, 1)) = visible(C, 1)$. Similarly we define a strategy of player 0 of $M$ on input $x$ to be a function $\tau$ mapping histories visible to player 0 on input $x$ into configurations visible to player 0 with the property that if $H$ is a history such that $last(H)$ is not a coin-tossing configuration and $player(H) = 0$ then then $HC$ is a history where $C$ is a configuration such that $\sigma(visible(H, 0)) = visible(C, 0)$.

**Example 2.2** *Consider the game automaton introduced in the previous example. A strategy $\sigma$ of player 1 is given in Table 2.2.*

| $visible(H, 1)$ | $\sigma(visible(H, 1))$ |
|---|---|
| $(init, 0), (init, 1)$ | $(h, 1)$ |
| $(init, 0), (init, 1), (h, 1)$ | $(hh, 0)$ |
| $(init, 0), (init, 1), (t, 1)$ | $(th, 0)$ |

Table 2.2: *Strategy $\sigma$ of player 1 of M, Example 2.2.*

## Markov Strategies

Markov strategies form a special subset of the strategies of a player. In a Markov strategy for player $i$, player $i$'s steps depend only on the current configuration of the game and not on the whole history of the game played so far. Thus a Markov strategy for player $i$ on input $x$ is a function mapping configurations visible to player $i$ to configurations visible to player $i$. More precisely, we say strategy $\sigma$ of player $i$ is a *Markov* strategy if for any histories $H_1$ and $H_2$, if $last(visible(H_1), i) = last(visible(H_2), i)$ then $\sigma(visible(H_1, i)) = \sigma(visible(H_2, i))$. Later we will see that in many instances we can restrict our attention to the Markov strategies of a player.

## 2.1.4 Computation Trees

A *computation tree* of $M$ on input $x$ is a (possibly infinite) labeled binary tree $T$ with the following properties.

1. Each node $\eta$ of the tree is labeled with a configuration $l(\eta)$ and the root of the tree has label $init(M, x)$. For a node $\eta$, if $l(\eta)$ is a universal, existential, coin-tossing, accepting or rejecting configuration we say $\eta$ is a universal, existential, coin-tossing accepting or rejecting node, respectively.

2. Every internal node $\eta$ has two children $\eta_1$ and $\eta_2$ such that

$$l(\eta) \to l(\eta_1) \text{ and } l(\eta) \to l(\eta_2) .$$

3. $\eta$ is accepting or rejecting if and only if $\eta$ is a leaf.

The sequence of configurations labeling nodes of any path from the root of the computation tree is a history.

## A Computation Subtree for Fixed Strategies of Both Players

To measure how good a fixed strategy $\sigma$ of player 1 is against some fixed strategy $\tau$ of player 0, we define tree $T_{\sigma,\tau}$ to be a subtree of $T$ with the following properties. Each universal node $\eta$ has one child $\eta_1$ such that if $H$ is the sequence of configurations labeling the nodes on the path from the root to $\eta$, then $\tau(visible(H, 0)) = visible(l(\eta_1), 0)$. Similarly, each existential node $\eta$ has one child $\eta_1$ such that if $H$ is the sequence of configurations labeling the nodes on the path from the root to $\eta$, then $\sigma(visible(H, 1)) = visible(l(\eta_1), 0)$. Each coin-tossing node of $T_{\sigma,\tau}$ has two children.

Each computation tree $T_{\sigma,\tau}$ has a *value* which is a measure of how good strategy $\sigma$ is against strategy $\tau$. For a tree $T_{\sigma,\tau}$ define the level, $level(\eta)$, of a node $\eta$ to be the distance of that node from the root. The root is at level 0. For each $k$ we define $value_{\sigma,\tau}(\eta, k)$ for each node $\eta$ in the tree as follows: if $level(\eta) \geq k$ then $value_{\sigma,\tau}(\eta, k) = 0$. Otherwise

$$value_{\sigma,\tau}(\eta, k) = \begin{cases} 0, \text{if } \eta \text{ is rejecting,} \\ 1, \text{if } \eta \text{ is accepting,} \\ \frac{1}{2}[value_{\sigma,\tau}(\eta_1, k) + value_{\sigma,\tau}(\eta_2, k)], \\ \qquad \text{if } \eta \text{ is coin-tossing with children } \eta_1, \eta_2, \\ value_{\sigma,\tau}(\eta_1, k), \\ \qquad \text{if } \eta \text{ is universal or existential with child } \eta_1 . \end{cases}$$

It is not difficult to see that for all nodes $\eta$ and all $k$:

$$value_{\sigma,\tau}(\eta, k) \leq value_{\sigma,\tau}(\eta, k+1) \leq 1.$$

So we define $value_{\sigma,\tau}(\eta) = \lim_{k \to \infty} value_{\sigma,\tau}(\eta, k)$.

The value of tree $T_{\sigma,\tau}$ is denoted by $v_{\sigma,\tau}$ and is equal to $value_{\sigma,\tau}(root(T_{\sigma,\tau}))$, where $root(T_{\sigma,\tau})$ is the root of $T_{\sigma,\tau}$. The next lemma describes the relationship between values of nodes in tree $T_\sigma$ and the values of their children.

**Lemma 2.1** *Let $\eta$ be a node of $T_{\sigma,\tau}$. Then*

$$
value_{\sigma,\tau}(\eta) = \begin{cases} \frac{1}{2}[value_{\sigma,\tau}(\eta_1) + value_{\sigma,\tau}(\eta_2)], \\ \quad \textit{if } \eta \textit{ is a coin-tossing node with children } \eta_1 \textit{ and } \eta_2, \\ value_{\sigma,\tau}(\eta_1), \\ \quad \textit{if } \eta \textit{ is an existential or a universal node with child } \eta_1. \end{cases}
$$

**Proof:** The proof follows immediately from the definition of the value of a node $\eta$ up to level $k$ as $value_{\sigma,\tau}(\eta, k)$, by taking the limit as $k \to \infty$. $\square$

There is an alternative way to define the value of a node $\eta$ in tree $T_{\sigma,\tau}$; it is the probability of reaching an accepting leaf, following a path from $\eta$ by choosing the successor of a coin-tossing node with equal probability from its two children. We prove next that this alternative definition of value is equivalent to the formal definition above. Later in the proofs of Chapters 3 and 4, we will see that both definitions of value are useful in different ways to argue about the value of particular strategies.

**Lemma 2.2** *Let $T_{\sigma,\tau}$ be a computation tree and let $\eta$ be any node of $T_{\sigma,\tau}$. Then*

$$
value_{\sigma,\tau}(\eta) = \text{Prob}[ \text{ an accepting leaf is reached from node } \eta] \,.
$$

**Proof:** We show that for any $k$,

$$
value_{\sigma,\tau}(\eta, k) = \sum_{j<k} \text{Prob}[ \text{ an accepting leaf at level } j \text{ is reached from node } \eta \,].
$$

$$(2.1)$$

The lemma follows by taking the limit as $k \to \infty$ of both sides of Equation 2.1. We prove Equation 2.1, by induction on $k - level(\eta)$. If $k - level(\eta) \leq 0$ the equation holds trivially, since both sides equal 0. Hence we consider the case when $k - level(\eta) > 0$. First suppose that $\eta$ is an existential or a universal node with child $\eta_1$. By induction, we can assume that

$$
value_{\sigma,\tau}(\eta_1, k) = \sum_{j<k} \text{Prob}[ \text{ an accepting leaf at level } j \text{ is reached from } \eta_1 \,],
$$

since $level(\eta_1) - k < level(\eta) - k$. Since $\eta_1$ is the only child of $\eta$, it follows that

$$value_{\sigma,\tau}(\eta, k) = value_{\sigma,\tau}(\eta_1, k)$$

$$= \sum_{j<k} \text{Prob[ an accepting leaf at level } j \text{ is reached from node } \eta_1 \text{ ]}$$

$$= \sum_{j<k} \text{Prob[ an accepting leaf at level } j \text{ is reached from node } \eta \text{ ]},$$

as required. The other case to consider is when $\eta$ is a coin-tossing node with children $\eta_1$ and $\eta_2$. Then

$$value_{\sigma,\tau}(\eta, k) = \tfrac{1}{2}(value_{\sigma,\tau}(\eta_1, k) + value_{\sigma,\tau}(\eta_2, k))$$

$$= \tfrac{1}{2}(\sum_{j<k} \text{Prob[an accepting leaf at level } j \text{ is reached from node } \eta_1 \text{ ]}$$

$$+ \sum_{j<k} \text{Prob[an accepting leaf at level } j \text{ is reached from node } \eta_2 \text{ ]}),$$

$$= \sum_{j<k} \text{Prob[an accepting leaf at level } j \text{ is reached from node } \eta \text{ ]},$$

as required. This completes the proof that both definitions of the value of a computation tree are equivalent. $\square$

The value of computation tree $T_{\sigma,\tau}$ is a measure of how good strategy $\sigma$ of player 1 is against a *particular* strategy $\tau$, of player 0. It does not give any indication of how good strategy $\sigma$ is against the best possible strategy of player 0. Let $M$ be a probabilistic game automaton and let $\mathcal{T}$ be the set of strategies of player 0 of $M$ on input $x$. Then for any strategy $\sigma$ of player 1 on $x$, we define

$$v_\sigma = \inf_{\tau \in \mathcal{T}} \{v_{\sigma,\tau}\} .$$

Value $v_\sigma$ measures how good strategy $\sigma$ is against the best possible strategy of player 0.

## A Computation Subtree for a Fixed Strategy of Player 1 when player 1 displays complete information

In many of the games we consider, we assume that player 1 always displays complete information. In this case, we define another subtree $T_\sigma$ of computation tree $T$ for each strategy $\sigma$ of player 1. We define values for nodes of this tree, and show that the value of the root equals $v_\sigma$, which is the value of $\sigma$ against the best possible strategy of player 0. This tree representation of strategies of player 1 when player 1 displays complete information will be useful in proofs later.

For every strategy $\sigma$ of player 1 on $x$, we define $T_\sigma$ to be a subtree of $T$ where every universal and coin-tossing node has two children and every existential node $\eta$ has exactly one child $\eta_1$. If $H$ is the sequence of configurations labeling nodes on the path from the root to $\eta$ then $\sigma(visible(H, 1)) = visible(l(\eta_1), 1)$. The value of a node $\eta$ of $T_\sigma$ is denoted by $value_\sigma(\eta)$. It is defined just as the value of $T_{\sigma,\tau}$, except the value of a universal node equals the *minimum* of the values of its two children.

**Example 2.3** *A computation tree.*

We describe the computation tree corresponding to strategy $\sigma$ defined in Table 2.2 for the game automaton of our example. Recall that in this game automaton player 1 displays complete information and player 0 takes no universal steps. The computation tree $T_\sigma$ is illustrated in Figure 2.2, and has value $\frac{1}{4}$. It is not hard to see that no strategy of player 1 has value greater than $\frac{1}{4}$. Suppose that the game had been defined differently so that player 0's coin-tosses are visible to player 1. A game automaton $M'$ which simulates this game is similar to $M$ except that player 0 of $M'$ has no private substates and the visible substate of $M'$ is a pair whose components are the private and visible substates of $M$. A strategy $\sigma'$ of player 1 of $M'$ is listed in Table 2.3, and the corresponding computation tree $T_{\sigma'}$ in Figure 2.2, has value 1. Thus, not surprisingly, player 1 gains an advantage when player 0 does not hide its coin-tosses.

Just as for the values of nodes of $T_{\sigma,\tau}$, there is a natural relationship between the values of nodes of $T_\sigma$ and their children. This relationship is given in Lemma 2.3.

| $visible(H,1)$ | $\sigma'(visible(H,1))$ |
|---|---|
| $(init, init, 0), (a, init, 0),$ $(ab, init, 1),\ \ a, b \in \{h, t\}$ | $(ab, a, 1)$ |
| $(init, init, 0), (a, init, 0), (ab, init, 1),$ $(ab, a, 1),\ \ a, b \in \{h, t\}$ | $(ab, ab, 0)$ |

Table 2.3: *Strategy $\sigma'$ of player 1 of $M'$, Example 2.3.*

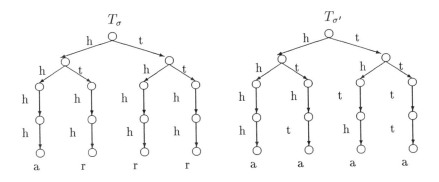

Figure 2.2: *Computation trees $T_\sigma$ and $T_{\sigma'}$, Example 2.3.*

**Lemma 2.3** *Let $\eta$ be a node of $T$. Then*

$$value_\sigma(\eta) = \begin{cases} \frac{1}{2}[value_\sigma(\eta_1) + value_\sigma(\eta_2)], \\ \quad \textit{if } \eta \textit{ is coin-tossing with children } \eta_1, \eta_2, \\ \min\{value_\sigma(\eta_1), value_\sigma(\eta_2)\}, \\ \quad \textit{if } \eta \textit{ is universal with children } \eta_1, \eta_2, \\ value_\sigma(\eta_1), \\ \quad \textit{if } \eta \textit{ is existential with child } \eta_1 \, . \end{cases}$$

**Proof:** The proof follows immediately from the definition of the value of a node $\eta$ of $T_\sigma$ up to level $k$, just as in Lemma 2.1. $\square$

We claim that $value_\sigma(root(T_\sigma))$ is $v_\sigma$, the value of strategy $\sigma$ against the best possible strategy $\tau$ of player 0. Recall that by definition, $v_\sigma = \inf\limits_{\tau \in \mathcal{T}} \{v_{\sigma, \tau}\}$.

In the following lemma we give a formal proof of this.

**Lemma 2.4** *Let $M$ be a probabilistic game automaton where player 1 displays complete information and let $T$ be the set of strategies of player 0 of $M$ on input $x$. Then for any strategy $\sigma$ of player 1 on $x$,*

$$value_\sigma(root(T_\sigma)) = \inf_{\tau \in T} \{v_{\sigma,\tau}\} \ .$$

**Proof:** Fix an input $x$ and let $\tau$ be any strategy of player 0 on $x$. We first show that for any node $\eta$ in tree $T_{\sigma,\tau}$, $value_\sigma(\eta) \leq value_{\sigma,\tau}(\eta)$, for all $\tau \in T$. (Note that since $T_{\sigma,\tau}$ is a subtree of $T_\sigma$, if $\eta$ is a node of tree $T_{\sigma,\tau}$ then it is also a node of tree $T_\sigma$ and so $value_\sigma(\eta)$ is well-defined). From this it follows that $value_\sigma(root(T_\sigma)) \leq \inf_{\tau \in T} \{v_{\sigma,\tau}\}$, since

$$value_\sigma(root(T_\sigma)) \leq value_{\sigma,\tau}(root(T_{\sigma,\tau})) = v_{\sigma,\tau} \ .$$

Secondly we show that there is some strategy $\tau_{opt}$ for which $value_\sigma(\eta) = value_{\sigma,\tau_{opt}}(\eta)$ for all nodes $\eta$ of tree $T_{\sigma,\tau}$. Finally we combine these two facts to prove the lemma.

Let $\eta$ be any node of tree $T_{\sigma,\tau}$. For any fixed $\tau \in T$, we prove that for any $k$, $value_\sigma(\eta, k) \leq value_{\sigma,\tau}(\eta)$. Taking the limit as $k \to \infty$ of both sides of this inequality, it follows that $value_\sigma(\eta) \leq value_{\sigma,\tau}(\eta)$. The proof of this is very similar to the proof of Lemma 2.2 and is done by induction on $k - level(\eta)$.

The basis case, when $k - level(\eta) \leq 0$, is trivial, since then $value_\sigma(\eta, k) = 0$. The case when $\eta$ is a leaf is also trivial. Hence suppose $k - level(\eta) > 0$ and that $\eta$ is not a leaf. Let $\eta_1$ and $\eta_2$ be the children of $\eta$ in tree $T$. We consider separately the cases where $\eta$ is coin-tossing, existential or universal. If $\eta$ is a coin-tossing node, then

$$\begin{aligned}
value_\sigma&(\eta, k) \\
&= \tfrac{1}{2}[value_\sigma(\eta_1, k) + value_\sigma(\eta_2, k)] \\
&\leq \tfrac{1}{2}[value_{\sigma,\tau}(\eta_1) + value_{\sigma,\tau}(\eta_2)], \text{ by the induction hypothesis,} \\
&= value_{\sigma,\tau}(\eta), \text{ by Lemma 2.1 .}
\end{aligned}$$

The case when $\eta$ is an existential node is similar. Finally suppose $\eta$ is a universal node. Without loss of generality assume that $\eta$ has child $\eta_1$ in $T_{\sigma,\tau}$.

Then

$$
\begin{aligned}
value_\sigma(\eta, k) \ &= \min\{value_\sigma(\eta_1, k), value_\sigma(\eta_2, k)\} \\
&\leq value_\sigma(\eta_1, k) \\
&\leq value_{\sigma,\tau}(\eta_1), \quad \text{(by the induction hypothesis)}, \\
&= value_{\sigma,\tau}(\eta), \quad \text{since the child of } \eta \text{ is } \eta_1 \text{ in } T_{\sigma,\tau} .
\end{aligned}
$$

This completes the proof that $value_\sigma(\eta) \leq value_{\sigma,\tau}(\eta)$.

We now show that there is some strategy $\tau_{opt}$ for which $value_{\sigma,\tau_{opt}}(\eta) \leq value_\sigma(\eta)$. Let $H$ be any history of $M$ on $x$ such that $last(H)$ is a universal configuration. First suppose there exists a node $\eta$ of $T_\sigma$ such that the path from $root(T_\sigma)$ to $\eta$ is labeled by history $H$. Let $\eta_1$ and $\eta_2$ be the children of $\eta$. Then

$$
\tau_{opt}(H) = \begin{cases} l(\eta_1), & \text{if } value_\sigma(\eta_1) \leq value_\sigma(\eta_2), \\ l(\eta_2), & \text{otherwise} . \end{cases}
$$

If such a node $\eta$ does not exist, $\tau_{opt}$ is defined arbitrarily. We now show that, for all nodes $\eta$ of $T_{\sigma,\tau_{opt}}$ and for all $k$,

$$
value_{\sigma,\tau_{opt}}(\eta, k) \leq value_\sigma(\eta) .
$$

We prove this by induction on $k - level(\eta)$. Taking the limit of this inequality as $k \to \infty$ immediately implies that $value_\sigma(\eta) \geq value_{\sigma,\tau_{opt}}(\eta)$. The basis case, when $k - level(\eta) \leq 0$, is trivial, since then $value_{\sigma,\tau_{opt}}(\eta, k) = 0$. The case when $\eta$ is a leaf is also trivial. Hence suppose that $k - level(\eta) > 0$ and that $\eta$ is not a leaf. Let $\eta_1$ and $\eta_2$ be the children of $\eta$ in tree $T$. We consider separately the cases where $\eta$ is coin-tossing, existential or universal. If $\eta$ is a coin-tossing node, then

$$
\begin{aligned}
value_{\sigma,\tau_{opt}}&(\eta, k) \\
&= \tfrac{1}{2}[value_{\sigma,\tau_{opt}}(\eta_1, k) + value_{\sigma,\tau_{opt}}(\eta_2, k)] \\
&\leq \tfrac{1}{2}[value_\sigma(\eta_1) + value_\sigma(\eta_2)], \quad \text{by the induction hypothesis}, \\
&= value_\sigma(\eta), \quad \text{by Lemma 2.3} .
\end{aligned}
$$

The case where $\eta$ is an existential node is similar. Finally suppose $\eta$ is a universal node. Without loss of generality assume that $value_\sigma(\eta_1) \leq value_\sigma(\eta_2)$. The other case, when $value_\sigma(\eta_1) > value_\sigma(\eta_2)$ is similar. Then from the definition of $\tau_{opt}$, $\eta_1$ is the child of $\eta$ in $T_{\sigma,\tau_{opt}}$, and so $value_{\sigma,\tau_{opt}}(\eta) = value_{\sigma,\tau_{opt}}(\eta_1)$.

We can now obtain the desired inequality:

$$value_{\sigma,\tau_{opt}}(\eta, k) = value_{\sigma,\tau_{opt}}(\eta_1, k)$$
$$\leq value_\sigma(\eta_1), \quad \text{by the induction hypothesis,}$$
$$= \min\{value_\sigma(\eta_1), value_\sigma(\eta_2)\}$$
$$= value_\sigma(\eta), \quad \text{by Lemma 2.3 .}$$

This completes the proof that $value_{\sigma,\tau_{opt}}(\eta) \leq value_\sigma(\eta)$. In particular,

$$v_\sigma = value_\sigma(root(T_\sigma)) \geq value_{\sigma,\tau_{opt}}(root(T_{\sigma,\tau})) .$$

Combining this with the fact that $value_\sigma(\eta) \leq value_{\sigma,\tau}(\eta)$, for all $\tau \in \mathcal{T}$, it follows that $v_\sigma = value_\sigma(root(T_\sigma))$, as required. $\square$

As a consequence of this lemma, we can denote by $v_\sigma$ the value of the root of a tree $T_\sigma$, which represents a strategy $\sigma$ of player 1 in a game automaton where player 1 displays complete information.

## 2.1.5   Language Acceptance

A strategy $\sigma$ is a *bounded winning strategy* for player 1 on input $x$ with bound $\epsilon > 0$ if the value of $\sigma$, denoted by $v_\sigma$, is $> \frac{1}{2} + \epsilon$. Similarly a strategy $\sigma$ is a *bounded losing strategy* for player 1 on input $x$ with bound $\epsilon > 0$, if $v_\sigma \leq \frac{1}{2} - \epsilon$. A probabilistic game automaton $M$ is a *bounded random* game automaton if there is $\epsilon > 0$ (depending only on $M$) with the property that, for any input $x$, either player 1 has a bounded winning strategy with bound $\epsilon$ or every strategy of player 1 is a bounded losing strategy with bound $\epsilon$. The *error probability* of a game automaton with bound $\epsilon < \frac{1}{2}$ is $\frac{1}{2} - \epsilon$. Let $M$ be a bounded random game automaton with bound $\epsilon$. Then the *language accepted* by $M$ is

$$L(M) = \{x : \text{ player 1 of } M \text{ has a bounded winning strategy on } x \}.$$

An *unbounded* winning (or losing) strategy is defined as for a bounded winning (or losing) strategy except $\epsilon \geq 0$. A probabilistic game automaton $M$ is an *unbounded random* game automaton if it has the property that, for any input $x$, either player 1 has an unbounded winning strategy or every strategy of player 1 is an unbounded losing strategy. Let $M$ be an unbounded random game automaton. Then the language accepted by $M$ is $L(M) = \{x : \text{ player 1 of } M \text{ has an unbounded winning strategy on } x\}$. Clearly, any language accepted by a bounded random game automaton is also accepted by an unbounded random game automaton.

## 2.1.6   Time, Space and History Bounds

There are different possibilities for defining time and space bounds. We could consider average time and space or time and space bounds which occur with very high probability. For simplicity we consider only *worst case time and space bounds* and leave a study of the other possibilities for the future. A computation tree is *t time bounded* if the longest path from the root to a leaf is bounded by $t$. A computation tree is *s space bounded* if each configuration in the tree contains at most $s$ work tape cells. Clearly a time bounded computation tree must be finite, but a space bounded computation tree could possibly be infinite.

A game automaton is $t(n)$ *time bounded* ($s(n)$ *space bounded*) if for every $n$, all strategies of the players on each input of length $n$ yields a computation tree which is $t(n)$ time bounded ($s(n)$ space bounded). A function $f(n)$ is *time (space) constructible* if there is a deterministic Turing machine which on each input of length $n$ runs in exactly $t(n)$ time (visits exactly $s(n)$ tape cells) and halts. In all of the results of this thesis about time and space bounded game automata we assume that the time and space bounds are constructible. Because we are only considering time and space bounds that are constructible we could have, without loss of generality, placed our time and space bounds only on winning strategies of player 1. Almost all of the results on game automata in this thesis depend on the fact that the time and space bounds are constructible; however it may be possible to remove this restriction from the space bounded results.

Another resource we measure is the amount of *history* on which a strategy of player 1 depends. We say a strategy $\sigma$ of player 1 on input $x$ has *history bound h* if $\sigma(visible(H_1, 1)) = \sigma(visible(H_2, 1))$ for any pair of histories of $M$ on $x$ such that the sequence consisting of the last $h$ visible configurations of $visible(H_1, 1)$ and the corresponding sequence of $visible(H_2, 1))$ are the same. Intuitively, the strategy $\sigma$ depends only on the last $h$ configurations of the history visible to player 1. Clearly if $\sigma$ is a Markov strategy then $\sigma$ has history bound 1. We say game automaton $M$ with bound $\epsilon$ is $h(n)$ history bounded if for any input of length $n$ accepted by $M$, there is a strategy $\sigma$ of player 1 of $M$ which has history bound $h(n)$ and is a bounded winning strategy of $M$ on $x$ with bound $\epsilon$, that is, $v_\sigma > \frac{1}{2} + \epsilon$. For all inputs $x$ rejected by $M$, all strategies $\sigma$ of player 1 on $x$ have value $v_\sigma \leq \frac{1}{2} - \epsilon$, including strategies whose histories are not bounded by $h(|x|)$. If $M$ has history bound 1 then we say $M$ is a *Markov game automaton*. Equivalently, $M$ is a Markov game automaton if for every input accepted by $M$, some Markov strategy of player 1 is a winning strategy.

### 2.1.7   A Restricted Model

The preceding sections give definitions and basic notation to describe a general two person computational game. In the rest of the thesis we do not consider this general model, but a restricted model where player 1 has no private heads, tapes or substates. We consider this restricted model because it is simpler and is still general enough to encompass all of the models already studied in the literature, and more. It is an open problem whether the results of this thesis, which apply only to the model where player 1 has no private information, can be extended to the most general model. For the rest of the thesis, when we refer to a probabilistic game automaton, we mean one where player 1 displays complete information.

In a game automaton of complete or partial information, we can assume that player 1 takes no coin-tossing steps, that is, steps when the turn indicator is 1 and the current state is a coin-tossing state. All the coin-tossing steps for both players can be made by player 0. This is because of our assumption that player 1 displays complete information. Since all coin-tossing steps of player 1 are visible to player 0, player 0 can simply toss all the coins of the game.

## 2.2   Notation

Within this model of a probabilistic game automaton there are many different types of game automaton, where player 1 is existential and player 0 is restricted in some way. To describe the restrictions on player 0, we use the following notation. The symbol $\forall$ is used to denote that player 0 can make universal moves. If $M$ is an unbounded random game automaton, then the letter $U$ is used to denote that player 0 can take coin-tossing steps; if $M$ is a bounded random game automaton then the letter $B$ is used. Finally the letters $Z$, $P$ or $C$ are used to denote that player 0 displays zero, partial or complete information, respectively. Table 2.4 summarizes this notation.

| Universal moves | Coin-tossing steps | Degree of information |
|:---:|:---:|:---:|
| $\forall$ | $U$ | $Z$ |
| | $B$ | $P$ |
| | | $C$ |

Table 2.4: *Notation used to classify probabilistic game automata.*

To specify the restrictions on player 0, $\forall$ is either chosen or not, at most of one of $U$ or $B$ is chosen, and exactly one of $Z$, $P$ or $C$ is chosen.

**Example 2.4**    *1. A $\forall BP$ automaton is a bounded random probabilistic game automaton where player 0 makes universal and coin-tossing moves and displays partial information. For a given input $x$, either player 1 has a bounded winning strategy on $x$ or all strategies of player 1 on $x$ are bounded losing strategies.*

   *2. A $\forall C$ automaton is a game automaton where player 0 can make universal moves but does not toss coins. Player 0 displays complete information. An automaton in the class $\forall C$ is in fact an alternating Turing machine (see Section 2.3).*

In general, a game automaton with complete information is a special case of a game automaton with partial information, namely the case where player 0 never uses its private tapes and heads. Similarly a game automaton with zero information is a special case of a game with partial information, where player 0 never uses its visible states and heads. For example, a game automaton in the class $UC$ is a special case of a game in the class $UP$, and a game automaton in the class $UZ$ is a special case of game in the class $UP$.

The suffixes $-TIME(t(n)), -SPACE(s(n)), -HIS(s(n))$ are used to restrict time, space and history. For any class of game automata $G$, $G-TIME(t(n))$ is the class of languages accepted by game automata of type $G$ that are $O(t(n))$ time bounded. Similarly, $G-SPACE(s(n))$ denotes the class of languages accepted by game automata of type $G$ that are $O(s(n))$ space bounded. Since a game automaton of complete or zero information is a special case of a game with partial information there are many trivial containments between the classes which can be defined by this notation. For example,

$$UC\text{--}TIME(t(n)) \subseteq UP\text{--}TIME(t(n)) \text{ and}$$

$$UZ\text{--}TIME(t(n)) \subseteq UP\text{--}TIME(t(n)) .$$

Other complexity classes that will be referred to in the paper are $BPP$ and $PP$, which are the classes of languages accepted by polynomial time probabilistic Turing machines with bounded and unbounded error probability, respectively. Also $BSPACE(s(n))$ denotes the class of languages accepted by $s(n)$ space bounded probabilistic Turing machines with bounded error probability. $poly(n)$ denotes the set of functions of the form $n^k$ for any integer $k$. $DTIME(t(n))$,, $DSPACE(s(n))$ denote the class of languages accepted by a deterministic Turing machine that is $t(n)$ time bounded or $s(n)$ space bounded, respectively. $PSPACE$ refers to the class of languages accepted by deterministic Turing machines that use polynomial space. To refer to game automata with just a finite number of alternations between the players we use the prefix $\Sigma_k$- to denote game automata with $k$ moves where player 1 makes the first move and $\Pi_k$ to denote game automata where player 0 makes the first move. For example, $\Sigma_k\text{--}UP\text{--}TIME(poly(n))$ is the class of languages accepted by unbounded random game automata with partial information that run in polynomial time where player 1 makes the first move and there are $k$ moves. As another example, $\Pi_1\text{--}UC\text{--}time(poly(n)) = \Pi_1\text{--}UP\text{--}time(poly(n)) = PP$, since in a game automaton from either of the classes $\Pi_1\text{--}UC$ or $\Pi_1\text{--}UP$, player 0 takes only coin-tossing steps and since player 1 never gets to move, there are no existential moves. Similarly, $\Pi_1\text{--}BC\text{--}time(poly(n)) = BPP$ and $\Pi_1\text{--}C\text{--}time(poly(n)) = P$. We use the standard notation $\Sigma_k^P$ and $\Pi_k^P$ to refer to the class of languages accepted by polynomial time bounded alternating Turing machines with $k$ alternations, or moves, where the first move is made by the existential player and the universal player, respectively.

# 2.3 Special Cases of Probabilistic Game Automata

We have now described a probabilistic game automaton and have defined a notation to refer to various types of probabilistic game automata. The purpose of this section is to describe in some detail some special types of game automata that have already proven useful in understanding problems in computer science. We also show how all of these models are special types of probabilistic game automaton, thus showing that the probabilistic game automaton provides a uniform framework in which to categorize and study these game automata.

## 2.3.1   Alternating Turing Machines

The alternating Turing machine of Chandra, Kozen and Stockmeyer [9] was the first game-like model of computation to be studied. An alternating Turing machine is a game between two players, called the existential player and the universal player. The players have complete information of the moves of the game; both players have strategies and neither player can toss coins. Chandra et al. studied such games that are time or space bounded. Many natural problems that have game-like characteristics can be formulated in terms of alternating Turing machines. For example, a prototypical language for the class of polynomial time bounded Turing machines is the True Quantified Boolean Formulas Problem. Let

$$TQBF = \{F = \exists x_1 \forall x_2 \ldots Q_k x_k (f(x_1, x_2, \ldots, x_k)) |$$

$$f \text{ is a boolean formula and } F \text{ is true} \} \ .$$

Given a quantified boolean formula, there is a natural two-person game between player 0 and player 1 such that player 1 always wins if the formula is in the language $TQBF$. In the game, the players take turns to choose values for the boolean variables $x_1, \ldots, x_k$ in that order. Player 1 chooses values for odd numbered variables and player 0 chooses values for even numbered variables. Once all variables have been assigned values, the game halts in an accepting state if the assignment satisfies the formula $f$; otherwise the game halts in a rejecting state.

It is not hard to see that the class of alternating Turing machines equals the class of game automata $\forall C$, in the notation of Section 2.2. The standard notation that is used to refer to the class of languages accepted by alternating Turing machines that are $t(n)$ time bounded or $s(n)$ space bounded is $ATIME(t(n))$ and $ASPACE(s(n))$, respectively. Tight relationships between time and space bounded alternating Turing machines and deterministic complexity classes were proved by Chandra et al. They showed that

$$NSPACE(s(n)) \subseteq ATIME(s^2(n)) \subseteq DSPACE(s^2(n)) \text{ and}$$

$$ASPACE(s(n)) = \cup_{c \geq 0} DTIME(2^{cs(n)}) \ .$$

## 2.3.2   Games Against Nature

A game against nature [27] is a two person game of complete information where one player makes moves at random, representing nature and the other, the existential player, moves according to a strategy. The input is accepted if the existential player has a strategy that wins against the random player with probability $> \frac{1}{2}$. Thus a game against nature is an unbounded random game and is in fact any game in the class $UC$.

Papadimitriou considered time bounded games against nature. He showed that the class $UC\text{--}TIME(poly(n))$ contains a large class of problems in optimization: decision problems under uncertainty. One example of a problem in this class is the stochastic scheduling problem. Suppose $t$ tasks are to be scheduled on $m$ processors so as to minimize the total time to execute all the tasks. There are precedence constraints among the tasks, which form a rooted in-tree, called a precedence tree. The execution times of the tasks are random variables with identical exponential distributions. The scheduling is done on-line as follows. First at most $m$ tasks that are at the leaves of the precedence tree are assigned processors. As soon as one task is completed, the other tasks are preempted, placed back on the precedence tree and $m$ new tasks are chosen to be scheduled. This procedure continues until all jobs are completed. The scheduling process can be thought of as a game against nature where player 1 chooses the best set of tasks to schedule and player 0 randomly chooses which job will halt first. The scheduling problem can be formulated as a language problem where the input consists of the number of tasks, the number of processors, the precedence tree, the expected running time of the tasks and a time limit $L$. The input is accepted if the tasks can be completed within time limit $L$, with probability $> \frac{1}{2}$.

Papadimitriou showed that $UC\text{--}TIME(poly(n)) = PSPACE$. This result has two interesting consequences. First, it helps categorize the complexity of decision problems under uncertainty such as the stochastic scheduling problem. Before Papdimitriou's work, it was not known that some of these problems had polynomial space solutions. Second, since it implies that $UC-TIME(poly(n)) = ATIME(poly(n))$, it shows that the class of languages accepted by polynomial time bounded two-player games with a 'disinterested' opponent is the same as the class of languages accepted by games with an 'interested' opponent. Later in Chapter 3, we study a closely related game model — the polynomial time bounded game automata in the class $UP$. This can be thought of as the class of games against *unknown* nature, since the existential player may have only partial information about what nature is computing.

### 2.3.3   Arthur-Merlin Games

Similar to games against nature are the Arthur-Merlin games described by Babai [2]. In an Arthur-Merlin game, Merlin wishes to prove something to Arthur, such as membership of an input in a language. Arthur can toss coins and accepts statistical evidence as proof. If Merlin can convince Arthur with high probability, then Merlin wins the game. An Arthur-Merlin game can be modeled as a bounded random probabilistic game automaton with complete information. Player 0 corresponds to Arthur and can toss coins, and player 1 corresponds to Merlin. Arthur-Merlin games and $BC$ games are equivalent.

Babai showed that some computational problems involving matrix groups such as membership and order have polynomial time bounded Arthur-Merlin games where each player takes just one turn. These problems are not known to be in $NP$. He also studied the hierarchy of time bounded Arthur-Merlin games where the players make a finite number of moves and proved that this hierarchy collapses.

### 2.3.4   Interactive Proof Systems

Goldwasser, Micali and Rackoff [19] considered the following question: what languages have efficient, that is, polynomial time, proofs? To formalize this question they introduced the model of an interactive protocol and an interactive proof system ($IPS$). We define these models, and the terminology associated with them, in terms of probabilistic game automata.

An *interactive protocol* is a two person computational game, similar to a probabilistic game automaton, with the following properties. Player 1 is called the *prover*, denoted by $P$, and player 0 is called the *verifier*, denoted by $V$. The interactive protocol is denoted by $(P, V)$. Neither $P$ nor $V$ have a strategy, both toss coins and both display partial information. The visible worktapes are of a special form. There are two of them and they are called *communication tapes*. One tape is used by $P$ to send messages to $V$. $P$ may only write on (and not read) this tape and $V$ is restricted to only read (and not write on) this tape. The other tape is used by $V$ to send messages to $P$ in a similar way. When the turn indicator changes to 1, the prover is said to be activated, and when the turn indicator changes to 0 the verifier is said to be activated. When the prover is activated, the contents of the communication tape which can be read by the prover is a *message sent* by the verifier to the prover. A message sent by the prover to the verifier is defined similarly. The interactive protocol is $t(n)$ *time bounded* if the number of steps taken by the verifier is $O(t(n))$. Note that the time used by the prover is not counted.

An interactive protocol $(P, V)$ is an *interactive proof system* for a language $L$ if there exists $\epsilon > 0$ such that

- for all $x \in L$, $(P, V)$ halts in an accepting state on $x$ with probability $> \frac{1}{2} + \epsilon$,

- for all $x \notin L$ and all interactive protocols $(P^*, V)$, $(P^*, V)$ halts in an accepting state on input $x$ with probability $\leq \frac{1}{2} - \epsilon$.

There are three important differences between interactive proof systems and probabilistic game automata. First, the prover of an interactive proof system cannot make existential moves whereas player 1 of a probabilistic game automaton can. Second, the time used by the verifier, and *not* the prover, is counted as the time used by an interactive proof system, whereas in a probabilistic game automaton, both the times used by the players 0 and 1 are counted. Third, the definition of language acceptance is different for interactive proof systems and probabilistic game automata.

Let *IPS–TIME*$(t(n))$ denote the class of languages for which there exist $t(n)$ time bounded interactive proof systems. Our goal is to show that

$$IPS\text{--}TIME(t(n)) = BP\text{--}TIME(t(n)) \,.$$

Before we can show this, we list some assumptions that can be made about interactive proof systems without loss of generality. The assumptions are as follows. First, on inputs of length $n$, all messages sent by either player are of length exactly $m$, where $m = O(t(n))$. Second, the last message sent from the verifier to the prover is a suitable encoding of 'accept' or 'reject', if the final state is accepting or rejecting, respectively. Third, the verifier is activated at the start of the protocol. Finally we assume that the worktape alphabet of the interactive proof system is binary.

For a fixed input $x$ and a $t(n)$ time bounded verifier $V$, we represent all possible communications of any prover with $V$ on $x$ by a tree which we call a *communication tree*. We denote the tree by $T_V$ and it has the following properties.

- The nodes of the tree are partitioned into $P$-nodes and $V$-nodes.

- All nodes at odd levels of the tree are $P$-nodes and all nodes at even levels are $V$-nodes (the root is at level 0).

- Each internal node $\eta$ has $2^m$ children, where $m$ is the length of a message. Also each child of $\eta$ is labeled by a distinct message, denoted by $message(\eta)$, where $|message(\eta)| = m$.

- Let $\eta_0, \ldots, \eta_{i-1}$ be a sequence of nodes on a path of the tree where $\eta_0$ is the root, $\eta_i$ is a $V$-node, and $\eta_k$ is the child of $\eta_{k-1}$, for $1 \leq k \leq i-1$. Let $\eta_i$ be any child of $\eta_{i-1}$. Then the edge from $\eta_{i-1}$ to $\eta_i$ is labeled by a probability $p_i$, where $p_i$ is the probability that the verifier sends message $message(\eta_i)$, given that messages $message(\eta_0), \ldots, message(\eta_{i-1})$ have been sent between the players so far.

Note that given the transition function for $V$, the tree can be constructed in time exponential in $t(|x|)$, and has depth $O(t(|x|))$. Also the probabilities labeling the outgoing edges from $V$-nodes can be written down in space polynomial in $t(|x|)$. This is because the verifier has to compute the probability in $t(|x|)$ steps. We assign a value to every node in tree $T_V$ as follows. A leaf has value 1 if it is labeled by an 'accept' message; otherwise its value is 0. Let $\eta$ be a $V$-node with children $\eta_1, \ldots, \eta_{2^m}$ and let the probability labeling the edge from $\eta$ to $\eta_i$ be $p_i$. Then $value(\eta) = \sum_{i=1}^{2^m} p_i value(\eta_i)$. Let $\eta$ be a $P$-node with children $\eta_1, \ldots, \eta_m$. Then $value(\eta) = \max_i \{value(\eta_i)\}$.

We claim that $value(root(T_V))$ is at least as great as the probability that $(P, V)$ accepts $x$, for *any* prover $P$. We outline the proof of this. Corresponding to any prover $P$ is a communication tree $T_{P,V}$ which has all the properties of $T_V$ plus one extra property:

- let $\eta_0, \ldots, \eta_{i-1}$ be a sequence of nodes of the tree where $\eta_0$ is the root, $\eta_{i-1}$ is a $P$-node and $\eta_k$ is a child of $\eta_{k-1}$, for $1 \leq k \leq i - 1$. Let $\eta_i$ be any child of $\eta_{i-1}$. Then the edge from $\eta_{i-1}$ to $\eta_i$ is labeled by a probability $p_i$, where $p_i$ is the probability that the prover $P$ sends message $message(\eta_i)$, given that messages $message(\eta_0), \ldots, message(\eta_{i-1})$ have been sent between the players so far.

Again we can associate a well-defined value with every node of $T_{P,V}$ in a natural way. The value of the leaves and the $V$-nodes are defined just as for tree $T_V$. The value of a $P$-node is defined differently. Let $\eta$ be a $P$-node of $T_{P,V}$ with children $\eta_1, \ldots, \eta_{2^m}$ and let the probability labeling the edge from $\eta$ to $\eta_i$ be $p_i$. Then $value(\eta) = \sum_{i=1}^{2^m} p_i value(\eta_i)$. It is straightforward to show that the value of $T_{P,V}$ equals the probability that $(P, V)$ accepts $x$ and that the value of $T_{P,V}$ is less than or equal to the value of $T_V$.

We now show that given an interactive proof system $(P, V)$ for language $L$, there is a prover $P'$ such that $(P', V)$ is an interactive proof system for $L$ and $P'$ is deterministic. $P'$'s protocol is as follows. When first activated on input $x$, $P'$ constructs the communication tree $T_V$ and computes the value of every node. $P'$ maintains a pointer, which points to various nodes of the tree $T_V$ during the execution of the protocol. Initially $P'$ sets the pointer to point to $root(T_V)$. At each activation of $P'$ (including its initial activation), $P'$ moves the pointer from the node to which it currently points, say $\eta_1$, to the child of that node which is labeled by the message just sent by $V$. Let this node be $\eta_2$. Then $P'$ moves the pointer again to the child of $\eta_2$ with greatest value. (If there is more than one such node, it decides arbitrarily which node to choose). Let this node be $\eta_3$. Finally to complete its turn, the prover writes $message(\eta_3)$ on its communication tape and activates the verifier. Again, it is straightforward to show that the probability $(P', V)$ accepts $x$ equals the value of the root of communication tree $T_V$, $value(root(T_V))$.

We show that $(P', V)$ accepts the same language $L$ as $(P, V)$. First suppose

$x \in L$. From our earlier observations and the definition of language acceptance,

$$\text{Prob}[(P', V) \text{ accepts } x] = value(root(T_V)) \geq \text{Prob}[(P, V) \text{ accepts } x] \geq \frac{1}{2} + \epsilon \, .$$

Hence $x$ is accepted by $(P', V)$. If $x \notin L$, then again from the definition of language acceptance of $(P, V)$, for any other interactive proof system $(P^*, V)$, $(P^*, V)$ halts in an accepting state on $x$ with probability $\leq \frac{1}{2} - \epsilon$. Hence $(P', V)$ is an interactive proof system for $L$.

We can now show that $IPS–TIME(t(n)) = BP–TIME(t(n))$. First, suppose $L$ is a language in the class $IPS–TIME(t(n))$ and let $(P, V)$ be a $t(n)$ time bounded interactive proof system for $L$, where $P$ is deterministic. We define a $t(n)$ time bounded game automaton $M$ in the class $BP$ which accepts $L$. The verifier $V$ is simulated by player 0 of $M$ and the prover $P$ is simulated by player 1. The problem with this is that player 1 cannot perform all the computations of the prover since this may take time more than $t(n)$. The idea is that player 1 simulates the prover $P$ by existentially writing on the visible tapes the messages from the prover to the verifier. Because it does this existentially, is does not have to do the computations of the prover which would lead to the same symbols being written on the tape. It can do this in $O(t(n))$ time since this is a bound on the length of the messages. Hence the running time of $M$ is $O(t(n))$. $M$ is a game of partial information since the verifier displays partial information, and hence player 0 displays partial information. Since the computation of player 0 is identical to that of the verifier, the probability that $M$ accepts $x$ when player 1's strategy is to simulate prover $P$ equals the probability that $(P, V)$ accepts $x$. Hence any input accepted by $(P, V)$ is accepted by $M$. Also if $x$ is not accepted by $(P, V)$ then for all provers $P^*$, the probability that $(P^*, V)$ halts in an accepting state on $x$ is at most $\frac{1}{2} - \epsilon$. Thus no matter what strategy player 1 uses, that is, no matter what $P^*$ it simulates, $M$ halts in an accepting state with probability at most $\frac{1}{2} - \epsilon$ and so $x$ is rejected by $M$. This shows that $M$ and $(P, V)$ accept the same language.

Conversely suppose $L$ is a language accepted by a $t(n)$ time bounded game automaton $M$ with bound $\epsilon$ in the class $BP$. We describe an interactive proof system $(P, V)$ for language $L$ which runs in time $t(n)$. On any input $x$, player 0 of $M$ is simulated by the verifier $V$. Player 1 is simulated by the prover. However, the prover cannot take existential steps. Thus to determine which step to take at any time when player 1 would take an existential step, the prover must examine all strategies of player 1 from that step to the end of the game, and determine which strategy is best. To do this, it constructs the computation tree for each strategy; the computation tree with greatest value yields the best strategy. It can do this since it has no time limit and the computation trees can be constructed in a straightforward way in time exponential in $t(n)$. The verifier can simulate the steps of player 0, since player 0 uses time $t(n)$ and makes no universal moves. As well as simulating the moves of player 0, the verifier checks after each step of the prover that the prover is properly following player 1's transition function. The verifier can do this since player 1 of $M$ displays complete information and hence the prover also displays complete information. If the verifier notices that the prover deviates from the transition function of player 1, then the verifier immediately halts in a rejecting state.

If $x \in L$, the prover simulates a strategy of player 1 which has value $> \frac{1}{2} + \epsilon$ and hence the verifier halts in an accepting state with probability $> \frac{1}{2} + \epsilon$. However if $x \notin L$, no prover $P^*$ exists for which $(P^*, V)$ accepts $x$ with probability $\geq \frac{1}{2} - \epsilon$. To see this, note that the prover $P^*$ can either simulate a strategy of player 1, using the transition function of player 1, or it can deviate from the transition function of player 1. If the prover $P^*$ simulates a strategy of player 1, an accepting state is reached with probability $\leq \frac{1}{2} - \epsilon$ since every strategy of player 1 of $M$ is a bounded losing strategy with bound $\epsilon$. The prover $P^*$ cannot increase the probability of reaching an accepting state by deviating from the transition function of player 1, since the verifier checks that $P^*$ is properly following player 1's transition function. Hence $x$ is not accepted by $(P^*, V)$, for any prover $P^*$.

The verifier $V$ runs in time $O(t(n))$ since player 0 does; hence the time bound of $(P, V)$ is $O(t(n))$. Thus interactive proof systems and bounded random games with the same time bounds are equivalent.

It is not hard to see that any problem in $NP$ has an interactive proof. For example, if $SAT$ is the set of satisfiable formulas, the prover can prove that $f \in SAT$ by writing a satisfying assignment for the variables of $f$ on a visible tape. The verifier can check that the assignment written by the prover does satisfy the formula $f$ and accepts if and only if it does. Note that the verifier does not even use randomness or hide any information from the prover. An interesting example of a language not known to be in $NP$ but which has an interactive proof is *Graph Non-isomorphism*: the set of pairs of graphs $(G_1, G_2)$ which are not isomorphic. Goldreich, Micali and Wigderson [18] gave an algorithm to show that graph non-isomorphism has an interactive proof. The algorithm is summarized in Figure 2.3; it has error probability $\frac{1}{2^k}$ where $k$ is some positive integer.

Input: Graphs $G_1$ and $G_2$

repeat $k$ times
        verifier: privately and randomly choose $x \in \{1,2\}$;
                randomly permute $G_x$ to obtain $G$ isomorphic to $G_x$;
                write $G$ on a visible tape;
        prover: write $x' \in \{1,2\}$ on a visible tape;
        verifier: if $x \neq x'$ then halt in a rejecting state;
endrepeat
verifier: halt in an accepting state.

Figure 2.3: *Interactive proof for the Graph Non-isomorphism problem.*

Intuitively, the reason that this proof works is that since the prover cannot see which graph is being permuted by the verifier, it can only guess correctly which of graphs $G_1$ or $G_2$ is isomorphic to $G$ if $G_1$ and $G_2$ are not isomorphic. Thus if $G_1$ and $G_2$ are not isomorphic, then there exists a strategy for the prover such that the game will always halt in an accepting state. This strategy is simply to let $x'$ be the unique $x$ such that $G$ is isomorphic to $G_x$. However if the graphs are isomorphic, the probability the prover always gives the correct $x$ on $k$ rounds of the repeat loop is at most $\frac{1}{2^k}$. Interesting relationships between time bounded Arthur-Merlin games and interactive proof systems are summarized at the start of Chapter 3.

## 2.4  Properties of Probabilistic Game Automata

To complete this chapter, we prove two properties of probabilistic game automata. The first, Theorem 2.5, shows that the probabilistic game automaton is a reasonable model of computation in that it accepts the recursively enumerable sets. In this theorem, and in all other theorems in future chapters, we will make good use of the notation defined in Section 2.2.

**Theorem 2.5** *The probabilistic game automata accept exactly the recursively enumerable sets.*

**Proof:** Clearly any recursively enumerable set is accepted by some probabilistic game automaton, since deterministic Turing machines are a special case of probabilistic game automata, namely where only one player moves and behaves deterministically. Any recursively enumerable set is accepted by a deterministic Turing machine and hence by a probabilistic game automaton.

Conversely suppose $M$ is a probabilistic game automaton with bound $\epsilon$. The language accepted by $M$ is accepted by a deterministic Turing machine that runs the algorithm of Figure 2.4 on input $x$.

> $k \leftarrow 1$;
> repeat
> > construct $k$ levels of the computation tree of $M$ on $x$
> > for every strategy $\sigma$ of player 1;
> > let $v = \max_{\sigma}\{value_\sigma(root(T_\sigma), k)\}$;
> > $k \leftarrow k + 1$;
> until $v > \frac{1}{2} + \epsilon$;
> halt in an accepting state.

Figure 2.4: *Deterministic simulation of a probabilistic game automaton.*

For any input $x$ accepted by $M$, there is some strategy $\sigma$ of $M$ on $x$ such that $v_\sigma > \frac{1}{2}$. Since $v_\sigma = lim_{k \to \infty} value_\sigma(root(T_\sigma), k)$, and the sequence $\{value_\sigma(root(T_\sigma), k)\}$ is monotonically increasing, there is some integer $k$ such that $x$ is accepted by $M$ if and only if $value_\sigma(root(T_\sigma), k) > \frac{1}{2}$. Hence the deterministic Turing machine executing the algorithm of Figure 2.4 will eventually halt and accept on inputs $x$ accepted by $M$. If $x$ is not accepted by $M$ then the deterministic Turing machine never halts on input $x$ and so $x$ is rejected by the deterministic Turing machine. $\square$

Secondly we prove a result about game automata with complete information that will be useful in later chapters. We show that in a game with complete information, if player 1 has a strategy with value $v$ then some *Markov* strategy of player 1 has value $v$. Intuitively, the reason that this is the case is that in a game of complete information, what player 1 knows about what player 0 is doing is completely captured in the current configuration of the game. The result is not true for game automata of partial information because in that case, what player 1 knows about what player 0 is doing may depend on the whole history of the game.

**Theorem 2.6** *If $M$ is a probabilistic game automaton with complete informa- tion $M$ is a Markov game.*

**Proof:** Let $M$ be a game automaton with bound $\epsilon$. Fix an input $x$ that is accepted by $M$. We wish to show that some Markov strategy of player 1 of $M$ on $x$ is a winning strategy with bound $\epsilon$. The proof is done in a few stages. First, we define a strategy, which we call $\sigma_{opt}$, for player 1 of $M$ on $x$. Second, we argue that strategy $\sigma_{opt}$ is a Markov strategy. Thirdly, we argue that its value is at least as great as the value of *any* strategy of player 1 on $x$. Finally we combine the results of these stages to prove the theorem.

Let $T$ be the computation tree of $M$ on $x$. Before we can define $\sigma_{opt}$, we need to associate a value with every node of $T$. For each non-negative integer $k$ we define $value_{opt}(\eta, k)$ for each node $\eta$ in the tree as follows. If $level(\eta) \geq k$ then $value_{opt}(\eta, k) = 0$. Otherwise if $\eta$ is a leaf then $value_{opt}(\eta)$ is 0 if $\eta$ is rejecting and is 1 if $\eta$ is accepting. Otherwise let $\eta_1$ and $\eta_2$ be the children of $\eta$. Then

$$value_{opt}(\eta, k) = \begin{cases} \frac{1}{2}[value_{opt}(\eta_1, k) + value_{opt}(\eta_2, k)], & \text{if } \eta \text{ is coin-tossing,} \\ \min\{value_{opt}(\eta_1, k), value_{opt}(\eta_2, k)\}, & \text{if } \eta \text{ is universal,} \\ \max\{value_{opt}(\eta_1, k), value_{opt}(\eta_2, k)\}, & \text{if } \eta \text{ is existential.} \end{cases}$$

Let $value_{opt}(\eta) = \lim_{k \to \infty} value_{opt}(\eta, k)$. The value $value_{opt}(\eta)$ is well-defined for any $\eta$ since it is the limit of a non-decreasing sequence of numbers, all of which are bounded above by 1. We show that the value $value_{opt}(\eta)$ of a node $\eta$ of $T$ depends only on the configuration $l(\eta)$ labeling $\eta$.

**Claim 2.7** *Let $\eta$ and $\eta'$ be two nodes of $T$ such that $l(\eta) = l(\eta')$. Then $value_{opt}(\eta) = value_{opt}(\eta')$.*

**Proof:** Let $level(\eta) - level(\eta') = c$ and without loss of generality assume that $c \geq 0$. Since $l(\eta) = l(\eta')$, the subtrees rooted at $\eta$ and $\eta'$ are identical. Based on this fact, it is not hard to show by induction on $k$ that $value_{opt}(\eta, k) = value_{opt}(\eta', c + k)$ for all $k$, Taking the limit as $k \to \infty$ of both sides of this equality, it follows that $value_{opt}(\eta) = value_{opt}(\eta')$, as required. $\square$

We now construct strategy $\sigma_{opt}$, using the values $value_{opt}(\eta)$ just defined. Let $H$ be any history of $M$ on $x$ such that $last(H)$ is an existential configuration. Since $M$ is a game of complete information, $visible(H, 1) = H$ and so we define $\sigma_{opt}$ on history $H$ instead of $visible(H, 1)$. Let $\eta$ be any node of $T$ such that the path from $root(T)$ to $\eta$ is labeled by history $H$. Let $\eta_1$ and $\eta_2$ be the children of $\eta$. Then

$$\sigma_{opt}(H) = \begin{cases} l(\eta_1), & \text{if } value_{opt}(\eta_1) \geq value_{opt}(\eta_2), \\ l(\eta_2), & \text{otherwise .} \end{cases}$$

**Claim 2.8** *Strategy $\sigma_{opt}$ is a Markov strategy.*

**Proof:** We need to show that $\sigma_{opt}(H) = \sigma_{opt}(H')$, for any histories $H$ and $H'$ of $M$ such that $last(H) = last(H')$ and $last(H)$ is an existential configuration. Fix two such histories $H$ and $H'$. Let $\eta$ be a node of $T$ such that the path from $root(T)$ to $\eta$ is labeled by history $H$. Let $\eta_1$ and $\eta_2$ be the children of $\eta$. Similarly let $\eta'$ be a node of $T$ such that the path from $root(T)$ to $\eta'$ is labeled by history $H'$. Let $\eta_1'$ and $\eta_2'$ be the children of $\eta'$. Note that $l(\eta) = l(\eta') = last(H)$ and for $i \in \{1, 2\}$, $l(\eta_i) = l(\eta_i')$. Hence by Claim 2.7, $value_{opt}(\eta_i) = value_{opt}(\eta_i')$ for $i \in \{1, 2\}$.

By definition of $\sigma_{opt}$, if $\sigma_{opt}(H) = l(\eta_1)$ then $value_{opt}(\eta_1) \geq value_{opt}(\eta_2)$. Thus it is also the case that $value_{opt}(\eta_1') \geq value_{opt}(\eta_2')$. Hence $\sigma_{opt}(H') = l(\eta_1') = l(\eta_1) = \sigma_{opt}(H)$. Similarly if $\sigma_{opt}(H) = l(\eta_2)$ then $\sigma_{opt}(H) = \sigma_{opt}(H')$. Therefore $\sigma_{opt}(H) = \sigma_{opt}(H')$, as required. $\square$.

It remains to show that the value of $\sigma_{opt}$ is at least as great as the value of any other strategy of player 1 on input $x$. Let $\sigma$ be an arbitrary strategy of player 1 on $x$. We will prove that $v_\sigma \leq value_{opt}(root(T)) \leq v_{\sigma_{opt}}$. The bulk of this proof is divided into two claims. In Claim 2.9 we show that for any node $\eta$ in $T_\sigma$, $value_\sigma(\eta) \leq value_{opt}(\eta)$. Note that since $value_{opt}(\eta)$ is defined for all nodes $\eta$ in computation tree $T$, it is defined in particular for nodes in subtree $T_\sigma$. In Claim 2.10, we show that for any node $\eta$ in $T_{\sigma_{opt}}$, $value_{opt}(\eta) \leq value_{\sigma_{opt}}(\eta)$. Combining these inequalities when $\eta$ is $root(T)$ shows that

$$v_\sigma = value_\sigma(root(T_\sigma)) \leq value_{opt}(root(T)) \leq value_{\sigma_{opt}}(root(T_{\sigma_{opt}})) = v_{\sigma_{opt}} .$$

**Claim 2.9** *For any node $\eta$ of $T_\sigma$, $value_\sigma(\eta) \leq value_{opt}(\eta)$.*

**Proof:** Fix a node $\eta$ of $T_\sigma$. We prove by induction on $k - level(\eta)$ that $value_\sigma(\eta, k) \leq value_{opt}(\eta)$ for all $k$. Taking the limit of this inequality as $k \to \infty$ immediately implies the claim. The basis case, when $k - level(\eta) \leq 0$, is trivial, since then $value_\sigma(\eta, k) = 0$. The case when $\eta$ is a leaf is also trivial. Hence suppose that $k - level(\eta) > 0$ and that $\eta$ is not a leaf. Let $\eta_1$ and $\eta_2$ be the children of $\eta$ in tree $T$. We consider separately the cases where $\eta$ is coin-tossing, existential or universal. If $\eta$ is a coin-tossing node, then

$$\begin{aligned} value_\sigma(\eta, k) &= \tfrac{1}{2}[value_\sigma(\eta_1, k) + value_\sigma(\eta_2, k)] \\ &\leq \tfrac{1}{2}[value_{opt}(\eta_1) + value_{opt}(\eta_2)], \quad \text{by the induction hypothesis,} \\ &= value_{opt}(\eta) . \end{aligned}$$

The last equality follows by taking the limit as $k \to \infty$ of the definition $value_{opt}(\eta, k) = \tfrac{1}{2}[value_{opt}(\eta_1, k) + value_{opt}(\eta_2, k)]$.

The cases where $\eta$ is a universal or an existential node are similar. Hence for all $k$, $value_\sigma(\eta, k) \leq value_{opt}(\eta)$, as required. $\square$

**Claim 2.10** *For any node $\eta$ in $T_{\sigma_{opt}}$, $value_{opt}(\eta) \leq value_{\sigma_{opt}}(\eta)$.*

**Proof:** The proof of this claim is similar to the proof of Claim 2.9. Let $\eta$ be any node of $T_{\sigma_{opt}}$. We show that $value_{opt}(\eta, k) \leq value_{\sigma_{opt}}(\eta)$ for any $k \geq 0$. Taking the limit as $k \to \infty$ of this inequality, the claim follows immediately. We prove this by induction on $k - level(\eta)$. The basis case, when $k - level(\eta) \leq 0$ is trivial since then $value_{opt}(\eta, k) = 0$. The case when $\eta$ is a leaf is also trivial. Hence suppose that $k - level(\eta) > 0$ and that $\eta$ is not a leaf. Let $\eta_1$ and $\eta_2$ be the children of $\eta$ in $T$. We consider separately the cases where $\eta$ is coin-tossing, existential or universal. If $\eta$ is a coin-tossing node, then

$$
\begin{aligned}
value_{opt}(\eta, k) &= \\
&\tfrac{1}{2}[value_{opt}(\eta_1, k) + value_{opt}(\eta_2, k)] \\
&\le \tfrac{1}{2}[value_{\sigma_{opt}}(\eta_1) + value_{\sigma_{opt}}(\eta_2)], \text{ (by the induction hypothesis)}, \\
&= value_{\sigma_{opt}}(\eta).
\end{aligned}
$$

The case where $\eta$ is a universal node is similar. Finally suppose $\eta$ is an existential node. Without loss of generality assume that $value_{opt}(\eta_1) \ge value_{opt}(\eta_2)$. The other case, when $value_{opt}(\eta_1) < value_{opt}(\eta_2)$ is similar. Then from the definition of $\sigma_{opt}$, $\eta_1$ is the child of $\eta$ in $T_{\sigma_{opt}}$. We can now obtain the desired inequality:

$$
\begin{aligned}
value_{opt}(\eta, k) &= \max\{value_{opt}(\eta_1, k), value_{opt}(\eta_2, k)\} \\
&\le value_{opt}(\eta_1, k) \\
&\le value_{\sigma_{opt}}(\eta_1), \text{ by the induction hypothesis}, \\
&= value_{\sigma_{opt}}(\eta) , \text{ by Lemma 2.3 .}
\end{aligned}
$$

□

It follows immediately from the above claims that

$$
v_\sigma = value_\sigma(root(T_\sigma)) \le value_{opt}(root(T)) \le value_{\sigma_{opt}}(root(T_{\sigma_{opt}})) = v_{\sigma_{opt}} .
$$

Thus $\sigma_{opt}$ is a winning strategy with bound $\epsilon$ on $x$ if $\sigma$ is. Hence if player 1 has a winning strategy with bound $\epsilon$ on $x$, it has a winning Markov strategy with bound $\epsilon$ on $x$, completing the proof of the theorem. □

# 3

---

# Time Bounded Game Automata

This chapter is a study of probabilistic game automata that are time bounded. The complexity of bounded random game automata has previously received much attention, hence the main focus of this chapter is unbounded random game automata. Polynomial time bounded game automata in the class $UP$ is one class of game automata that has not previously been studied. The definition of this class, which we call *games against unknown nature*, extends the definition of the class of polynomial time games against nature just as the definition of interactive proof systems extends the definition of Arthur-Merlin games. We also consider time bounded classes of game automata with complete information that combine universal, existential and coin-tossing moves.

We show that for time bounded game automata that are unbounded random, partial information and randomness do not significantly increase the complexity of the games. Specifically we show that a game in the class $UP$, that runs in time $t(n)$ can be simulated by an alternating Turing machine, that is, a game with complete information and no randomness, in time $t^2(n)$. In the other direction, time bounded alternating Turing machines can be simulated by unbounded random game automata with the same time bound. The following two formulas summarize the results of Sections 3.1 and 3.2.

For time constructible $t(n)$,

$$ATIME(t(n)) \subseteq UC\text{--}TIME(t(n)),$$

$$\forall UC\text{--}TIME(t(n)) \subseteq ATIME(t(n) \log t(n)) \text{ and}$$

$$UC\text{--}TIME(t(n)) \subseteq UP\text{--}TIME(t(n)) \subseteq UC\text{--}TIME(t^2(n)) .$$

As a direct corollory of these results, we get the following result on bounded random game automata with complete information.

$$ATIME(t(n)) \subseteq \forall BC\text{--}TIME(t(n)) \subseteq ATIME(t(n)\log t(n)) \ .$$

The only classes that seem to be less powerful than alternating Turing machines are the classes of bounded random game automata where player 0 makes no universal moves, that is, the classes $BC\text{--}TIME(t(n))$ and $BP\text{--}TIME(t(n))$. Before getting to our results on unbounded random game automata, we summarize here some results already known about bounded random game automata. Babai [2] introduced the class $BC$, which he called Arthur-Merlin games (see Section 2.3.3). He considered polynomial time bounded Arthur-Merlin games with a constant number of alternations between the players and showed that these games can be simulated by polynomial time bounded Arthur-Merlin games with just one alternation; that is, a games with two moves, the first move being Arthur's (player 0's). Using the notation of Chapter 2, this implies that for all $k \geq 3$,

$$\textstyle\prod_k\text{--}BC\text{--}TIME(poly(n)) \cup \sum_k\text{--}BC\text{--}TIME(poly(n)) = \prod_2\text{--}BC\text{--}TIME(poly(n)).$$

Goldwasser and Sipser [20] studied polynomial time bounded Arthur-Merlin games and interactive proof systems and showed that

$$BP\text{--}TIME(poly(n)) = BC\text{--}TIME(poly(n)) \ .$$

One interesting application of this result is that any language that has an interactive proof can be proved to a verifier that displays complete information to the prover. This seems surprising at first since the interactive proof of the graph non-isomorphism problem described in Section 2.3.4 depends on the fact that the verifier can hide information from the prover. Finally, Aiello, Goldwasser and Hastad [1] considered the question whether a polynomial time bounded Arthur-Merlin game could be simulated by a polynomial time bounded Arthur-Merlin game with just a finite number of alternations between the players. They conjecture that this is not possible and show that there exists an oracle $A$ such that

$$(BC\text{--}TIME(poly(n)))^A \neq (\textstyle\prod_2\text{--}BC\text{--}TIME(poly(n)))^A \ .$$

# 3.1  Time Bounded Game Automata with Complete Information

In this section we relate unbounded random time bounded game automata with complete information with time bounded alternating Turing machines. Some relationships between these two models have already been proven. Papadimitriou [27], showed that the set of languages accepted by polynomial time bounded games against nature is the same as the set of languages accepted by polynomial time bounded alternating Turing machines. His results showed that for time constructible $t(n)$,

$$ATIME(t(n)) \subseteq UC\text{--}TIME(t(n)) \subseteq ATIME(t^2(n)) \ .$$

Yap [32] generalized this to show that $\forall UC\text{--}TIME(t(n)) \subseteq ATIME(t^2(n))$. M. Tompa suggested an improvement to Yap's result to obtain the tighter result that $\forall UC\text{--}TIME(t(n)) \subseteq ATIME(t(n) \log t(n))$. This result is presented in Theorem 3.2.

First we show in Lemma 3.1 how to simulate any $t(n)$ time bounded game automaton $M$ in the class $\forall UC$ by one in the same class that has a more uniform structure. This lemma will be used in the proof of Theorem 3.2.

**Lemma 3.1** *Let $t(n)$ be time constructible. If $M$ is a $t(n)$ time bounded game automaton in the class $\forall UC$ then there is a $O(t(n))$ time bounded game automaton $M'$ in the same class such that $M'$ accepts the same language as $M$ and for any input $x$,*

- *All full histories of $M'$ on $x$ are of the same length.*

- *Steps numbered $3k-2$ of $M'$ on $x$ are coin-tossing, $3k-1$ are existential and $3k$ are universal for any positive integer $k$ less than or equal to the running time of $M'$ on $x$.*

**Proof:** Let $x$ be an arbitrary input. The idea is that $M'$ 'pads' a computation of $M$ on $x$ by taking 3 steps for every step of $M$. One step simulates the step of $M$ and the other two steps are null steps. Steps $3k-2, 3k-1$ and $3k$ correspond to step $k$ of $M$. For example, to simulate an existential step of $M$, player $0'$ of $M'$ simulates a null coin-tossing step, then player $1'$ simulates the existential step followed by a null universal step of player $0'$. Then $M'$ accepts the same language as $M$ and the steps of $M'$ alternate between existential, coin-tossing and universal as required.

To ensure that all histories of $M'$ are of the same length, $M'$ counts the length of the history it is simulating. Let $ct(n)$ be an upper bound on the running time of $M'$ and let $m = ct(|x|)$. If $M'$ is about to enter a halting state before $3m$ steps, $M'$ takes null steps, alternating between existential, coin-tossing and universal steps until $3m$ steps have passed and then enters the halting state. $\square$

We now show that a $t(n)$ time bounded game of complete information can be simulated by a game with complete information that has time bound $O((t(n))$ and in which neither player makes coin-tossing moves.

**Theorem 3.2** *For time constructible* $t(n)$,

$$\forall UC\text{--}TIME(t(n)) \subseteq ATIME(t(n) \log t(n)) \ .$$

**Proof:** Let $M$ be a $t(n)$ time bounded game automaton in the class $\forall UC$, and assume that $M$ satisfies the properties of Lemma 3.1. To prove the theorem, we first show how to assign values to the nodes of computation tree $T$ of $M$ on an input $x$, such that the value assigned to the root of $T$ is $> \frac{1}{2}$ if and only if $x$ is accepted by $M$. Based on the tree $T$, we then show how to define a two-person game played by an existential and a universal player. In the game, the existential player has a winning strategy on $x$ if and only if the value of the root of $T$ is $> \frac{1}{2}$. Finally we show that this game can be played by the players of an alternating Turing machine that runs in time $O(t(n) \log t(n))$.

Fix an input $x$ and let $T$ be the computation tree of $M$ on $x$. Let $value(\eta)$, the value of node $\eta$ of $T$, be defined as follows.

$$
value(\eta) = \begin{cases}
\max\{v(\eta_1), v(\eta_2)\}, & \\
\quad \text{if } \eta \text{ is an existential node with children } \eta_1, \eta_2, & \\
\min\{v(\eta_1), v(\eta_2)\}, & \\
\quad \text{if } \eta \text{ is a universal node with children } \eta_1, \eta_2, & \\
\frac{1}{2}[v(\eta_1) + v(\eta_2)], & \\
\quad \text{if } \eta \text{ is a coin-tossing node with children } \eta_1, \eta_2, & \\
0, \text{ if } \eta \text{ is a rejecting node }, & \\
1, \text{ if } \eta \text{ is an accepting node }.
\end{cases}
$$

Since $M$ is time bounded, player 1 has only a finite number of possible strategies $\sigma$ on $x$. Thus $\max_{\sigma}\{v_\sigma\}$ exists, and using techniques similar to those in Section 2.1.3, it is not hard to see that $\max_{\sigma}\{v_\sigma\}$ equals the value of the root of $T$, as defined above. Hence the value of the root of $T$ is $> \frac{1}{2}$ if and only if $x$ is accepted by $M$. Note that the value of a node of $T$ lies between 0 and 1. If $level(\eta) = i$ then $value(\eta) = y_\eta/2^{m-i}$, where $y_\eta$ is an integer and $m$ is the depth of $T$. $M$ accepts $x$ if and only if $y_{root(T)} > 2^{m-1}$. To avoid dealing with fractions, we will use the values $y_\eta$ instead of $value(\eta)$ for each node $\eta$ of $T$ in the rest of the proof. Let $\eta$ be an arbitrary internal node of $T$ with children $\eta_1$ and $\eta_2$ and let $level(\eta) = i$. We derive an expression for $y_\eta$ in terms of $y_{\eta_1}$ and $y_{\eta_2}$. Since $value(\eta) = y_\eta/2^{m-i}$, $value(\eta)2^{m-i} = y_\eta$. Similarly, $value(\eta_i)2^{m-i+1} = y_{\eta_i}$ for $i = 1, 2$. Combining these equalities with the definition of $value(\eta)$, it follows that

$$
y_\eta = \begin{cases}
2\max\{y_{\eta_1}, y_{\eta_2}\}, & \text{if } \eta \text{ is an existential node,} \\
2\min\{y_{\eta_1}, y_{\eta_2}\}, & \text{if } \eta \text{ is a universal node,} \\
y_{\eta_1} + y_{\eta_2}, & \text{if } \eta \text{ is a coin-tossing node }.
\end{cases}
\tag{3.1}
$$

We now define a complete information game between an existential player (player 1) and a universal player (player 0) such that the existential player has a strategy that wins against any strategy of the universal player if and only if the value $y_{root}$ of the root of $T$ is $> 2^{m-1}$. The game goes as follows. First player 1 existentially chooses the value $y_{root}$. If the value chosen is $\leq 2^{m-1}$ then player 0 halts the game in a rejecting state. Otherwise the players verify that the value guessed by player 1 is actually the value of the root. The players can recursively verify that the value of a node $\eta$ is $y_\eta$, as follows. If $\eta$ is a leaf then $y_\eta = 1$ if $\eta$ is labeled by an accepting configuration and is 0 otherwise. If

$\eta$ is not a leaf, let the children of $\eta$ be $\eta_1$ and $\eta_2$. Player 1 existentially chooses the values $y_{\eta_1}$ and $y_{\eta_2}$ of the children of $\eta$. Player 0 checks that $y_\eta$, $y_{\eta_1}$ and $y_{\eta_2}$ satisfy the relation of Equation 3.1. Also player 0 universally chooses one child and recursively checks the value of that child.

However, this algorithm runs in time $O(t^2(n))$ since on an input of length $n$, at every step, a value of length $t(n)$ is written on a tape and there are $O(t(n))$ steps since the depth of $T$ is $O(t(n))$. We derive an algorithm that runs in time $O(t(n)\log t(n))$ by getting the players to check *one digit* of the value of a node of $T$, rather than the whole value, at each step. Since each value $y_\eta$ of $T$ on $x$ has at most $m = O(t(|x|))$ digits, a digit can be uniquely specified by $O(\log t(|x|))$ bits. Thus the running time is reduced to $O(t(n)\log t(n))$. The procedure $verify(\eta, j, b)$, which is given in Figure 3.1, checks that the $j$th digit of $y_\eta$ is $b$. If the value of the root, $y_{root(T)}$, is greater then $2^{m-1}$ then the $m$th digit of $y_{root(T)}$ must be 1 and some other digit must be 1. Initially player 1 guesses a digit $d$ other than the $m$th digit of $y_{root(T)}$ which is 1, and player 0 universally checks that digits $m$ and $d$ are 1 using the recursive procedure *verify*. The game halts in an accepting state if and only if both digits are 1, that is, if and only if $M$ accepts $x$.

Finally we argue that this algorithm can be run in time $O(t(n)\log t(n))$ on an alternating Turing machine. As in the first algorithm, there are $t(n)$ levels of recursion; hence each level must run in time $O(\log t(n))$. The non-trivial steps are in showing that the players can check the following:

1. '$y_{\eta_i} \le y_{\eta_{3-i}}$' or '$y_{\eta_i} \ge y_{\eta_{3-i}}$' (lines 10,14), and

2. '$carry_{j-1}$ is the carry from adding the low-order $j-2$ bits of $y_{\eta_1}$ and $y_{\eta_2}$' (line 18).

To check that '$y_{\eta_i} \le y_{\eta_{3-i}}$' or '$y_{\eta_i} \ge y_{\eta_{3-i}}$', the players need to be able to check statements of the form $y_{\eta_1} \le y_{\eta_2}$. To do this, player 1 existentially chooses the leftmost digit, say $d$, where $y_{\eta_1}$ and $y_{\eta_2}$ differ, ($d$ is chosen to be 0 if $y_{\eta_1} = y_{\eta_2}$) and player 0 universally checks using the procedure *verify* that digit $d$ of $y_{\eta_1}$ is 0, digit $d$ of $y_{\eta_2}$ is 1 and that corresponding digits of $y_{\eta_1}$ and $y_{\eta_2}$ that have order greater than $d$ are the same. To check that $carry_{j-1}$ is the carry from the addition of the low order $j-2$ digits of $y_{\eta_1}$ and $y_{\eta_2}$, player 1 chooses at which bit, say $g$, the carry is generated. Then player 0 universally checks that

*verify*$(\eta, j, b)$   (verify that the *jth* digit of $y_\eta$ is $b$
                    (the least significant digit is numbered 1) )
   <u>if</u> $\eta$ is a halting node <u>then</u>
      player 0:  halt in an accepting state if
                 $((b = 1) \wedge (j = 1) \wedge \eta$ is accepting)  or
                 $((b = 0) \wedge ((j > 1) \vee \eta$ is rejecting));
                 otherwise halt in a rejecting state;
   <u>else</u> let $\eta_1$ and $\eta_2$ be the children of $\eta$;
   <u>if</u> $\eta$ is a $\forall$ node <u>then</u>
      player 1:  guess $i \in \{1, 2\}$ such that $y_{\eta_i} = \min\{y_{\eta_1}, y_{\eta_2}\}$;
      player 0:  universally  *verify*$(\eta_i, j - 1, b)$;
                 check that $y_{\eta_i} \leq y_{\eta_{3-i}}$;
   <u>if</u> $\eta$ is a $\exists$ node <u>then</u>
      player 1:  guess $i \in \{1, 2\}$ such that $y_{\eta_i} = \max\{y_{\eta_1}, y_{\eta_2}\}$;
      player 0:  universally  *verify*$(\eta_i, j - 1, b)$;
                 check that $y_{\eta_i} \geq y_{\eta_{3-i}}$;
   <u>if</u> $\eta$ is a coin-tossing node <u>then</u>
      player 1:  guess $y_{\eta_1, j-1}, y_{\eta_2, j-1}$ and *carry*$_{j-1}$;
      player 0:  universally  check that $y_{\eta_1, j-1} \oplus y_{\eta_2, j-1} \oplus carry_{j-1} = b$;
                 check that *carry*$_{j-1}$ is the carry from adding
                 the low-order $j - 2$ bits of $y_{\eta_1}$ and $y_{\eta_2}$;
                 *verify*$(\eta_1, j - 1, y_{\eta_1, j-1})$
                 *verify*$(\eta_2, j - 1, y_{\eta_2, j-1})$

Figure 3.1: *Algorithm to check one digit of the value of a node of computation tree $T$, Theorem 3.2.*

bit $g$ of $y_{\eta_1}$ and $y_{\eta_2}$ are 1, and that for $g < p < j - 2$, bit $p$ of $y_{\eta_1}$ or $y_{\eta_2}$ is 1, so that the carry is propagated.

This completes the proof that the algorithm runs in time $O(t(n) \log t(n))$ on an alternating Turing machine, and thus the proof of Theorem 3.2. $\square$

The relationship between time bounded game automata with complete information that have no randomness or are unbounded random is summarized in the next corollary.

**Corollory 3.3** *For time constructible $t(n)$,*

$$ATIME(t(n)) \subseteq UC\text{--}TIME(t(n)) \subseteq$$

$$\forall UC\text{--}TIME(t(n)) \subseteq ATIME(t(n) \log t(n)) \,.$$

**Proof:** The first containment, that $ATIME(t(n)) \subseteq UC\text{--}TIME(t(n))$, was proven by Papadimitriou [27]. The containment $UC\text{--}TIME(t(n)) \subseteq \forall UC\text{--}TIME(t(n))$ is trivial. The rightmost containment is proved in Theorem 3.2. $\square$

## 3.2 Time Bounded Game Automata with Partial Information

We now turn our attention to unbounded random game automata with partial information. Our main result, Theorem 3.5, proves that the class of languages accepted by polynomial time bounded games against nature is the same as the class of languages accepted by polynomial time bounded games against *unknown* nature. The proof technique is different than that used by Sipser and Goldwasser [20] for the bounded random case. Just as in Section 3.1, we start by proving a lemma that shows how to simulate a $t(n)$ time bounded game automaton $M$ in the class $UP$ by an automaton that has a more uniform structure.

**Lemma 3.4** *Let $t(n)$ be time constructible. Any $t(n)$ time bounded probabilistic game automaton $M$ in the class UP can be simulated by a game automaton $M'$ in the class UP which accepts the same language as $M$, is $O(t^2(n))$ time bounded and has the following properties.*

*1. The players of $M'$ alternate moves at every step.*

*2. All full histories of $M'$ are of the same length.*

**Proof:** The statement, and the proof, of this lemma are similar to Lemma 3.1. However, the simulation of Lemma 3.1 does not carry over directly to game automata with partial information. The problem with the simulation of Lemma 3.1 for a game with partial information is that there may exist distinct histories $H_1$, $H_2$ of $M$ such that $visible(H_1, 1) = visible(H_2, 1)$, but if $H_1'$ and $H_2'$ are the histories of $M'$ that simulate $H_1$, $H_2$ respectively, then $visible(H_1', 1) \neq visible(H_2', 1)$. Hence a strategy of player $1'$ may map $H_1'$ and $H_2'$ onto distinct configurations and may in this way increase the probability that $M'$ halts in an accepting state. To show how such histories $H_1$ and $H_2$ can exist, we define a *hidden sequence* of steps of $M$ to be a sequence $i, \ldots, j, i \leq j$ of steps of player 0 which has the following properties:

- the visible part of the configurations of $M$ at steps $i, \ldots, j$ are the same,

- if $M$ does not halt at step $j$, the visible part of the configuration at step $j$ is different from that of step $j + 1$ and

- if $i > 0$, the visible part of the configuration at step $i - 1$ is different from that at step $i$.

Let $H_1$ and $H_2$ be histories representing distinct hidden sequences of different lengths such that $visible(H_1) = visible(H_2)$. Then $|visible(H_1')| = |H_1'| \neq |H_2'| = |visible(H_2')|$ since $H_1'$ and $H_2'$ have different lengths. To overcome this problem, player $0'$ must pad all hidden sequences of player 0 to length $t(n)$ during the simulation by taking null steps at which it does not change the visible configuration. Then since player $1'$ cannot distinguish the null steps from the simulated steps, all histories of $M'$ which have the same visible part are indistinguishable to player $1'$. The padding procedure may square the running time of $M$ so that it runs in time $O(t^2(n))$.

The automaton $M'$ just constructed satisfies property 1 of the lemma. To ensure that $M'$ satisfies property 2, that is, all histories are of the same length, $M'$ counts the length of the history it is simulating. If $M'$ is about to enter a halting state before $ct^2(n)$ steps, where $c$ is an appropriately chosen constant, $M'$ takes null steps until $ct^2(n)$ steps have passed and then enters the halting state. $\square$

**Theorem 3.5** *If $t(n)$ is time constructible then*

$$UP\text{–}TIME(t(n)) \subseteq UC\text{–}TIME(t^2(n)).$$

**Proof:** The proof of this result is similar to a proof by Reif [30] on games without randomness. From the previous lemma we know that any game automaton in the class $UP$ which is $O(t(n))$ time bounded can be simulated by a game automaton $M$ in the class $UP$ for which every full history has length exactly $ct^2(n)$, for some constant $c$, and the players alternate turns at every step. Without loss of generality, assume that player 0 of $M$ takes the odd numbered steps and player 1 takes the even numbered steps. We construct a game automaton $M'$ in the class $UC$ which simulates $M$ and is $O(t^2(n))$ time bounded.

Fix an input $x$ and let $m = ct^2(|x|)$. Before we can describe $M'$, we show how a sequence of $m$ numbers, each of constant length, can represent a visible history of $M$. Given the visible configuration of $M$ on $x$ at time $k$, there is a constant number, $a$ (assumed to be a power of 2), of possible visible configurations of $M$ at time $k + 1$. This is because in changing the visible configuration in one step, a player of $M$ can only change the visible state, the visible tape head positions and the contents of a constant number of tape cells. The $a$ possible visible configurations can be ordered in a straightforward way so that any number $\alpha$, $1 \leq \alpha \leq a$, uniquely determines the $\alpha th$ possible next visible configuration from any given visible configuration.

Let $S = \{\alpha_1 \ldots \alpha_m \mid \alpha_i \in \{1, \ldots, a\}, 1 \leq i \leq m\}$. Each string $\alpha_1 \ldots \alpha_m \in S$ represents a sequence of visible configurations $VC_0 \, VC_1 \ldots VC_m$, where $VC_0$ is the initial visible configuration of $M$ and $VC_i$ is the $\alpha_i th$ possible visible configuration from $VC_{i-1}$. For $1 \leq j \leq m$ we say $\alpha_1 \ldots \alpha_j$ *represents a visible history* if there is a history $C_0 C_1 \ldots C_j$ of $M$ such that $visible(C_i) = VC_i, 0 \leq i \leq j$. A string $\alpha_1 \ldots \alpha_j$ is *valid* if it represents a visible history. The empty string is valid by definition. A string $\alpha_1 \ldots \alpha_m$ is $\exists$-*invalid* if for some even $j, 1 \leq j \leq m$, $\alpha_1 \ldots \alpha_{j-1}$ is valid but $\alpha_1 \ldots \alpha_j$ is not. Similarly a string $\alpha_1 \ldots \alpha_m$ is $\mathcal{R}$-*invalid* if for some odd $j, 1 \leq j \leq m$, $\alpha_1 \ldots \alpha_{j-1}$ is valid but $\alpha_1 \ldots \alpha_j$ is not. The set $S$ can be partitioned into valid, $\exists$-invalid and $\mathcal{R}$-invalid strings.

We now describe the simulation of $M$ on $x$ by $M'$. The simulation is done in two stages. In the first stage, the players of $M'$ write down on a worktape a sequence $\alpha_1 \ldots \alpha_m$ from the set $S$. If $\Delta$ is the worktape alphabet of $M$, then the worktape alphabet of $M'$ is $\Delta \cup \{1, \ldots, a\}$. The players write alternate numbers in the sequence. Player $0'$ randomly writes down the numbers $\alpha_i$ where $i$ is odd, since these numbers represent configurations reached from coin-tossing configurations. Similarly player $1'$ existentially writes down $\alpha_i$ where $i$ is even. After $m$ turns, a sequence $\alpha_1 \ldots \alpha_m$ is written on the worktape, where for odd $i$, $\alpha_i$ is written randomly by player $0'$ and for even $i$, $\alpha_i$ is written existentially by player $1'$. Each $\alpha_i$ is of constant length, and so the sequence can be written in time $O(m)$. Let $VC_0 \ldots VC_m$ be the visible sequence of configurations represented by $\alpha_1 \ldots \alpha_m$.

The idea of the second stage is that player $0'$ tries to simulate a complete history $C_0 C_1 \ldots C_m$ of $M$, such that $visible(C_i) = VC_i$, $0 \leq i \leq m$. Clearly this is only possible if $\alpha_1 \ldots \alpha_m$ is valid. Player $1'$ does not move in the second stage. Player $0'$ starts in the initial configuration of $M$. Suppose player $0'$ has simulated a history $C_0 \ldots C_{j-1}$ such that for $0 \leq i \leq j-1$, $visible(C_i) = VC_i$. Then player $0'$ has simulated the first $j - 1$ steps of a history of $M$ and is in configuration $C_{j-1}$. If $j$ is even, player $0'$ checks that $\alpha_1 \ldots \alpha_j$ is valid, given that $\alpha_1 \ldots \alpha_{j-1}$ is. It can do this in constant time. If $\alpha_j$ is not valid then the string $\alpha_1 \ldots \alpha_m$ is $\exists$-invalid and player $0'$ halts in a rejecting state. Otherwise player $0'$ changes the visible part of configuration $C_{j-1}$ to obtain a new configuration $C_j$ such that $visible(C_j) = VC_j$, the visible configuration represented by $\alpha_j$.

If $j$ is odd, player $0'$ simulates a coin-tossing step of $M$ from configuration $C_{j-1}$. Thus player $0'$ simulates a step of player $0$ of $M$. Let $C_j$ be the configuration of $M'$ after this step. Player $0'$ checks if $visible(C_j) = VC_j$. If not, player $0'$ halts, accepting with probability $\frac{1}{2}$. Otherwise player $0'$ continues to the next step of the simulation. If $j = m$ then player $0'$ halts, and enters an accepting state if and only if $state(C_m)$ is an accepting state.

This completes the description of $M'$. It is not hard to see that the running time of the automaton $M'$ described above is $O(t^2(n))$ since this is the running time of $M$. It remains to show that $M$ and $M'$ accept the same language. Informally, this is true because the strategy of player $1'$ is completely determined in the first stage and in the first stage, the players only agree on the visible history to be simulated. Fix an input $x$. The proof that $M'$ accepts $x$ if and only if $M$ does is organized as follows. We first define what it means for a strategy $\sigma'$ of player $1'$ on input $x$ to *simulate* a strategy $\sigma$ of player $1$. A strategy which satisfies this definition is called a simulating strategy. We show that if player $1'$ uses a simulating strategy then no string written by the players in the first stage of the simulation is $\exists$-invalid. We also show that if player $1'$ has an unbounded winning strategy, it has one which simulates a strategy of player 1. We then consider the strategies $\sigma'$ of $M'$ such that $\sigma'$ simulates some strategy $\sigma$ of player 1 and show that $\sigma'$ is an unbounded winning strategy if and only if $\sigma$ is. Thus $M'$ accepts $x$ if and only if $M$ does.

We consider strategies $\sigma'$ of player $1'$ as mappings from strings $\alpha_1 \ldots \alpha_{j-1}$. We say strategy $\sigma'$ of player $1'$ *simulates* strategy $\sigma$ of player 1 if

$$\sigma'(\alpha_1 \ldots \alpha_{j-1}) = \alpha_j \Leftrightarrow \sigma(VC_0 \ldots VC_{j-1}) = VC_j,$$

for any even $j$ and any valid prefix $\alpha_1 \ldots \alpha_j$ of a string of $S$ which represents visible configurations $VC_0 \ldots VC_j$.

If $\sigma'$ simulates some strategy $\sigma$, we say $\sigma'$ is a *simulating* strategy. If $\sigma'$ is a simulating strategy then when a valid string $\alpha_1 \ldots \alpha_{j-1}$ is written in the first stage where $j$ is even, player $1'$ writes $\alpha_j$ on the tape where $\alpha_1 \ldots \alpha_j$ is also valid. If $\alpha_1 \ldots \alpha_{j-1}$ is $\mathcal{R}$-invalid, it does not matter what $\alpha_j$ player $1'$ writes.

Let $S_{\sigma'}$ be the subset of strings of $S$ of the form $s = \alpha_1 \ldots \alpha_m$ which can be written in the first stage of some execution of $M'$ on $x$ when player $1'$ uses strategy $\sigma'$.

**Claim 3.6** *A strategy $\sigma'$ of player $1'$ is a simulating strategy if and only if $S_{\sigma'}$ has no $\exists$-invalid strings.*

**Proof:** First suppose $\sigma'$ simulates strategy $\sigma$ and suppose $s = \alpha_1 \ldots \alpha_m$ is an $\exists$-invalid string in $S_{\sigma'}$. We show that this leads to a contradiction. Let $VC_0 \ldots VC_m$ be the sequence of visible configurations represented by $\alpha_1 \ldots \alpha_m$. Then for some even $j$, $VC_0 \ldots VC_{j-1}$ is a visible history of $M$ and $VC_0 \ldots VC_j$ is not. However since $\sigma'$ simulates $\sigma$, it must be that $\sigma(VC_0 \ldots VC_{j-1}) = VC_j$, contradicting the fact that $VC_0 \ldots VC_j$ is not a visible history of $M$. To prove the other direction, suppose that $S_{\sigma'}$ has no $\exists$-invalid strings. We wish to show that $\sigma'$ is a simulating strategy. Let $\psi$ be an arbitrary strategy of player 1 of $M$. We claim $\sigma'$ simulates the strategy $\sigma$ defined as follows on visible history $VC_0 \ldots VC_{j-1}$ where $j$ is even.

$$\sigma(VC_0 \ldots VC_{j-1}) = \begin{cases} VC_j, \text{if } VC_0 \ldots VC_j \text{ is a visible history} \\ \qquad \text{represented by a prefix of a string in } S_{\sigma'} \\ \psi(VC_0 \ldots VC_{j-1}), \text{otherwise} \,. \end{cases}$$

First we show that $\sigma$ is a well-defined strategy. It is clearly well-defined on visible histories which are not represented by a prefix of a string in $S_{\sigma'}$, hence we need only consider the case when $VC_0 \ldots VC_{j-1}$ is represented by a prefix of a string of $S_{\sigma'}$. Suppose $s_1$ and $s_2$ are two distinct strings of $S_{\sigma'}$ such that the first $j-1$ numbers of each represent $VC_0 \ldots VC_{j-1}$ where $j$ is even. Then the $j$th numbers of $s_1$ and $s_2$ are the same. This is because the strategy $\sigma'$ can only depend on the first $j-1$ numbers $\alpha_1, \ldots, \alpha_{j-1}$ when writing the $j$th number $\alpha_j$. Thus $VC_j$ is unique and hence $\sigma$ is well-defined. It follows immediately from the definition of a simulating strategy that $\sigma'$ simulates $\sigma$.
$\square$

**Claim 3.7** *Let $x$ be any input of length $n$ and let $s = \alpha_1 \ldots \alpha_{j-1}\alpha_j \ldots \alpha_m$ and $s' = \alpha_1 \ldots \alpha_{j-1}\alpha_j' \ldots \alpha_m'$ be two strings with the same valid prefix $\alpha_1 \ldots \alpha_{j-1}$ such that $\alpha_1 \ldots \alpha_{j-1}\alpha_j$ is $\exists$-invalid. Then Prob[$M'$ accepts $x$ if $s$ is written in the first stage] $\leq$ Prob[$M'$ accepts $x$ if $s'$ is written in the first stage].*

**Proof:** This fact follows easily from the following observations. First, if $M'$ halts in the second stage after simulating a history of length $< j$, then since the first $j-1$ symbols of $s$ and $s'$ are identical, the probability of $M'$ accepts $x$ are identical if $s$ or $s'$ are written in the first stage. Second, if $M'$ halts in the second stage after simulating a history of length $\geq j$ when $s$ is written in the first stage, then the probability that $M'$ accepts $x$ is 0, since it detects that $s$ is $\exists$-invalid. $\square$

**Claim 3.8** *For any strategy $\sigma''$ of player $1'$ on $x$, there is always a simulating strategy $\sigma'$ which is at least as good, that is, $v_{\sigma'} \geq v_{\sigma''}$.*

**Proof:** Suppose $\sigma''$ is not a simulating strategy of player $1'$. We define a simulating strategy $\sigma'$ such that $S_{\sigma'}$ contains all the strings of $S_{\sigma''}$ which are not $\exists$-invalid. To see that such a strategy exists, let $\psi'$ be an arbitrary simulating strategy of player $1'$. We define $\sigma'$ as a function of strings $\alpha_1 \ldots \alpha_{j-1}$, where $j$ is even, as follows.

$$\sigma'(\alpha_1 \ldots \alpha_{j-1}) = \begin{cases} \alpha_j, \text{ if } \alpha_1 \ldots \alpha_j \text{ is not } \exists-\text{invalid} \\ \qquad \text{ and is the prefix of a string in } S_{\sigma''} \\ \psi'(\alpha_1 \ldots \alpha_{j-1}), \text{ otherwise .} \end{cases}$$

It is straightforward from the definition of $\sigma'$ to see that $S_{\sigma'}$ has no $\exists$-invalid strings; hence by Claim 3.6 $\sigma'$ is a simulating strategy. Also, by the construction of $\sigma'$, each string $s = \alpha_1\alpha_2\ldots\alpha_m$ of $S_{\sigma''}$, such that $\alpha_1\alpha_2\ldots\alpha_{j-1}$ is valid but $\alpha_1\alpha_2\ldots\alpha_j$ is $\exists$-invalid is replaced by a string $s' = \alpha_1\ldots\alpha_{j-1}\alpha'_j\ldots\alpha'_m$ in $S_{\sigma'}$ that is not $\exists$-invalid.

We now show that $v_{\sigma'} \geq v_{\sigma''}$. For any strategy $\beta'$, if player $1'$ uses strategy $\beta'$ then each sequence $s \in S_{\beta'}$ can be written in the first stage of $M'$ with equal probability. This is because all sequences $s$ are of equal length and exactly $\lceil\frac{m}{2}\rceil$ of the $\alpha_i$ are chosen randomly. Hence the probability that $M'$ accepts $x$ when player $1'$ uses strategy $\beta'$ is

$$v_{\beta'} = \frac{1}{\mid S_{\beta'} \mid} \sum_{s \in S_{\beta'}} \text{Prob}[M' \text{ accepts } x \text{ if } s \text{ is written in the first stage}].$$

It follows from the definition of $\sigma'$, $S_{\sigma'}$ contains all strings of $S_{\sigma''}$ which are not $\exists$-invalid. Also $|S_{\sigma'}| = |S_{\sigma''}| = a^{\lceil\frac{m}{2}\rceil}$ since for any given strategy of player $1'$, there are $a^{\lceil\frac{m}{2}\rceil}$ possible strings written in the first stage. Let $k = |S_{\sigma''} - S_{\sigma'}|$. Hence

$$v_{\sigma'} - v_{\sigma''} = 1/k(\sum_{(s,s')} \text{Prob}[M' \text{ accepts } x \text{ is } s \text{ is written in the first stage}]$$
$$-\text{Prob}[M' \text{ accepts } x \text{ is } s' \text{ is written in the first stage}],$$

where the sum is taken over all pairs $(s, s')$ such that $s$ is $\exists$-invalid and $s'$ replaces $s$ in $\sigma'$. From claim 3.7. every term in this sum is $ge0$. Hence $v_{\sigma'} \geq v_{\sigma''}$, as required. $\square$

By Claim 3.8, an optimal strategy of player $1'$ on any input is a simulating strategy. Let $\sigma'$ be a strategy of $M'$ on input $x$ which simulates $\sigma$. To complete the proof, we derive an expression for the value of $v_{\sigma'}$ in terms of $v_\sigma$.

**Claim 3.9** *If $\sigma'$ simulates $\sigma$ then*

$$v_{\sigma'} = \frac{1}{\mid S_{\sigma'} \mid}(v_\sigma - \frac{1}{2}) + \frac{1}{2}.$$

It follows immediately from this that $M'$ accepts $x$ if and only if $M$ does, since $v_{\sigma'} > \frac{1}{2}$ if and only if $v_\sigma > \frac{1}{2}$, and thus $\sigma'$ is an unbounded winning strategy if and only if $\sigma$ is. It remains to proof Claim 3.9.

**Proof of Claim 3.9:** Since $M$ satisfies the properties of Lemma 3.4, the paths in the computation tree $T_\sigma$ are of equal length and are followed with equal probability. The sequence of labels of each path of $T_\sigma$ is a history of $M$. The paths of $T_\sigma$ can be partitioned into equivalence classes, where two paths are in the same equivalence class if the visible history labeling each of them is equal. Each string $s$ written in the first stage of $M'$ defines a visible history of $M$. For any string $s \in S_{\sigma'}$, let $p_s$ be the fraction of paths of $T_\sigma$ which are in the equivalence class corresponding to the visible history represented by $s$. Let $q_s$ be the fraction of paths in this equivalence class which are accepting. Then the probability of reaching an accepting leaf, following a path from the root of $T_\sigma$, is $v_\sigma = \sum_{s \in S_{\sigma'}} p_s q_s$.

Let $m$ be the depth of $T_\sigma$. Each path of length $m$ starting at the root of $T_{\sigma'}$ corresponds to a string $s \in S_{\sigma'}$. If $s$ is valid or $\mathcal{R}$-invalid we say the corresponding path is valid or $\mathcal{R}$-invalid, respectively. (Since $\sigma'$ is a simulating strategy, we can assume that $S_{\sigma'}$ has no $\exists$-invalid paths). Each path labeled by a valid string represents a visible history of $M$.

There is a one-to-one correspondence between the valid paths of $T_{\sigma'}$ and the equivalence classes of paths of $T_\sigma$. If a path of $T_{\sigma'}$ corresponds to string $s$, the subtree $T_s$ rooted at its $m$th node has one path for each path in the equivalence class corresponding to string $s$. Altogether, a fraction $p_s$ of the paths of $T_s$ correspond to paths in the equivalence class. Of the other paths of the subtree, the probability of reaching an accepting leaf is $\frac{1}{2}$.

In Figure 2 there is an example of two computation trees $T_\sigma$ and $T_{\sigma'}$. The paths of length $m$ from the root of $T_{\sigma'}$ labeled with 'a' are accepting and with 'r' are rejecting. Two equivalence classes of paths of $T_\sigma$ are shown, which correspond to valid paths of $T_{\sigma'}$. The fraction of leaves marked with $\bullet$ (respectively $\star$) which are accepting is $q_{s_1} = 3/4$ (respectively $q_{s_2} = 1/3$). The path labeled $s_3$ is $\mathcal{R}$-invalid, hence the probability of reaching an accepting leaf from the root of $T_{s_3}$ is $\frac{1}{2}$.

It follows from this that $p_s q_s + (1 - p_s)\frac{1}{2}$ is the probability of reaching an accepting leaf from the root of the subtree $T_s$. Thus

$$v_{\sigma'} = \frac{1}{|S_{\sigma'}|} \sum_{s \in S_{\sigma'}} \left(p_s q_s + (1 - p_s)\frac{1}{2}\right) = \frac{1}{|S_{\sigma'}|}(v_\sigma - \frac{1}{2}) + \frac{1}{2} ,$$

since $\sum_s p_s = 1$ and $v_\sigma = \sum_s p_s q_s$. This completes the proof of Claim 3.9. $\square$

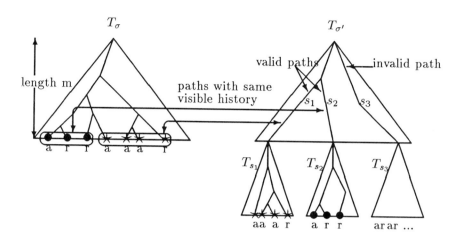

Figure 3.2: *Computation trees $T_\sigma$ and $T_{\sigma'}$, Theorem 3.5.*

It is an open problem whether this result can be extended to game automata where player 0 makes universal moves, that is, to the class $\forall UP$. Is $\forall UP\text{–}TIME(poly(n)) = ATIME(poly(n))$?

The following corollary unifies the results on time bounded game automata.

**Corollary 3.10** *For time constructible $t(n)$,*

$$ATIME(t(n)) \subseteq \forall BC\text{–}TIME(t(n)) \subseteq$$

$$\forall UC\text{–}TIME(t(n)) \subseteq ATIME(t(n)\log t(n)) \text{ and}$$

$$ATIME(t(n)) \subseteq UP\text{–}TIME(t(n)) \subseteq ATIME(t^2(n)) \; .$$

**Proof:** All the containments are immediate, except $\forall UC\text{–}TIME(t(n)) \subseteq ATIME(t^2(n)\log t(n))$ and $UP\text{–}TIME(t(n)) \subseteq ATIME(t^2(n)\log t(n))$. These follow from Theorems 3.2 and 3.5. □

Finally, we state the relationship between polynomial time bounded game automata in the following corollary.

**Corollory 3.11**

$$ATIME(poly(n)) = \forall UC\text{--}TIME(poly(n))$$

$$= \forall BC\text{--}TIME(poly(n)) = UP\text{--}TIME(poly(n)) \ .$$

**Proof:** Immediate from Corollory 3.10. $\square$

# 4

---

# Space Bounded Game Automata with Complete Information

In the next two chapters we consider space bounded probabilistic game automata. Although much work has been done on time bounded game automata previously, this work is the first detailed study of space bounded game automata. We prove a number of interesting results on space bounded game automata which show that they contrast with the results on time bounded game automata. The next chapter deals with game automata with partial information; in this chapter we concentrate on game automata with complete information. We consider $s(n)$ space bounded games against nature and Arthur-Merlin games. In our notation the classes of languages accepted by these games are $UC\text{--}SPACE(s(n))$ and $BC\text{--}SPACE(s(n))$, respectively. Our main result is that for space constructible $s(n) = \Omega(\log n)$,

$$BC\text{--}SPACE(s(n)) = UC\text{--}SPACE(s(n)) = ASPACE(s(n)) \,.$$

Thus Arthur-Merlin games and games against nature with the same space bound are equivalent. Both accept the class of languages $\cup_{c>0} DTIME(2^{cs(n)})$, since Chandra, Kozen and Stockmeyer have shown that for $s(n) = \Omega(\log n)$,

$$ASPACE(s(n)) = \cup_{c>0} DTIME(2^{cs(n)}) \,.$$

Recall that the difference between these models is that Arthur-Merlin games have error probability bounded away from $\frac{1}{2}$ whereas games against nature do not.

The techniques used to prove this result are different from those used to prove results on time bounded automata. The fact that $ASPACE(s(n)) \subseteq BC\text{–}SPACE(s(n))$, proved in Section 4.3, contrasts with the case for time bounded game automata, since it is unlikely that for any time constructible function $t(n)$, $ATIME(t(n)) \subseteq BC\text{–}TIME(poly(t(n)))$. We use results on Markov decision processes to prove that $UC\text{–}SPACE(s(n)) \subseteq ASPACE(s(n))$. This proof is done in Section 4.4. The main result stated above follows from these two results, since trivially $BC\text{–}SPACE(s(n)) \subseteq UC\text{–}SPACE(s(n))$.

Some building blocks for the proof of the main results are presented in Sections 4.1 and 4.2. One problem in analyzing space bounded probabilistic game automata is that they may not halt on some computations. Thus the computation tree representing a game may be infinite. In Section 4.1 we describe a graph representation for space bounded game automata that is similar to the computation tree representation of these game automata but has the advantage of being finite. In Section 4.2 we use this representation to show that it can be assumed without loss of generality that $s(n)$ space bounded game automata of complete information halt with probability 1 and in fact run in expected time $2^{2^{O(s(n))}}$.

It is interesting to note that all the results of this chapter depend on the fact that all game automata of complete information are Markov game automata (see Theorem 2.6). None of the results of this chapter extend to space bounded game automata of partial information.


# 4.1   Graph Representation

We have seen in Chapter 2 that any game automaton $M$ on input $x$ can be represented by a computation tree. If $M$ has space bound $s(n)$ with $s(n) = \Omega(\log n)$, the corresponding tree may have an infinite number of nodes on some inputs, although the number of distinct configurations labeling the nodes of the tree is bounded by $d^{s(n)}$, for some constant $d$. The graph representation of an $s(n)$ space bounded game automaton with complete information which we are about to describe has the advantage of having a finite number, at most $d^{s(n)}$, of nodes.

Let $M$ be an $s(n)$ space bounded game automaton with complete information. Without loss of generality assume that $M$ has a unique accepting and a unique rejecting configuration. We associate with $M$ on input $x$ of length $n$ a directed graph $G$, having at most $d^{s(n)}$ nodes, for some constant $d$, where each node is labeled by a distinct configuration of $M$. Let $\{1, \ldots, N\}$ be the nodes of $G$. There is an edge from node $i$ to node $j$ in the graph if there is a transition from the configuration labeling node $i$ to the configuration labeling node $j$ in $M$. The nodes labeled by accepting or rejecting configurations are called *halting* nodes. Each other node of the graph is either coin-tossing, existential or universal, depending on the configuration that labels it. All nodes except halting nodes have exactly two outgoing edges; for technical reasons we assume that each halting node $i$ has exactly one reflexive edge $(i, i)$. We call the node labeled by the initial configuration the *start* node and denote it by $start(G)$.

Consider a subgraph of $G$ obtained by removing one of the two edges from each existential node and each universal node of $G$. The set of remaining outgoing edges from the existential (universal) nodes of the subgraph is called an *existential policy* $\sigma$ (*universal policy* $\tau$) of $G$. We denote the subgraph as $G_{\sigma,\tau}$. There is a one-to-one correspondence between the Markov strategies of player 1 (player 0) of $M$ on input $x$ and the existential (universal) policies of $G$; hence we use the same symbols to refer to each of them. It will be clear from the context whether the strategy $\sigma$ or the policy $\sigma$ is meant. $G_{\sigma,\tau}$ can be considered as a Markov process where the states of the process are the nodes of $G$ and the transition probabilities $p_{ij}, 1 \leq i, j \leq n$ are defined as follows. If $i \leq n - 1$ then $p_{ij} = \frac{1}{2}$ if $i$ is a coin-tossing node with outgoing edge $(i, j)$; $p_{ij} = 1$ if $i$ is an existential or universal node with outgoing edge $(i, j)$ and $p_{ij} = 0$ otherwise. Since $N - 1$ and $N$ are halting states, we define $p_{NN} = p_{N-1N-1} = 1$, $p_{Nj} = 0$ if $j \neq N$ and $p_{N-1j} = 0$ if $j \neq N - 1$.

We define the *value* $v_{\sigma,\tau}(i)$ of each vertex $i$ of $G$ with respect to policies $\sigma$ and $\tau$ to be the probability of reaching the accepting node from the start node on a random walk of the Markov process $G_{\sigma,\tau}$, starting from vertex $i$. Without loss of generality, let nodes $1, \ldots, k$ be the nodes of $G_{\sigma,\tau}$ with a path to a halting node, excluding the halting nodes themselves. Then clearly the values $v_{\sigma,\tau}(i), 1 \leq i \leq N$ satisfy the following conditions. If $k < i \leq N - 1$ then $v_{\sigma,\tau}(i) = 0$ and $v_{\sigma,\tau}(N) = 1$; otherwise

$$v_{\sigma,\tau}(i) = \begin{cases} \frac{1}{2}(v_{\sigma,\tau}(j) + v_{\sigma,\tau}(k)), & \text{if } i \text{ is a coin-tossing node of } G_{\sigma,\tau} \\ & \text{with outgoing edges } (i,j), (i,k), \\ v_{\sigma,\tau}(j), & \text{if } i \text{ is an existential or universal node} \\ & \text{of } G_{\sigma,\tau} \text{ with outgoing edge}(i,j). \end{cases}$$

$$(4.1)$$

We next show that the equations (4.1) have a unique solution.

**Lemma 4.1** *Let $G$ be a graph representation of a space bounded game automaton where $G$ has $N$ nodes. Suppose that nodes $1, \ldots, k$ are the nodes of $G_{\sigma,\tau}$ with a path to a halting node, excluding the halting nodes themselves. Let $\vec{v}_{\sigma,\tau} = (v_{\sigma,\tau}(1), \ldots, v_{\sigma,\tau}(k))$. Then there is a $k \times k$ matrix $Q$ and a $k$-vector $\bar{b}$ with entries in $\{0, 1/2, 1\}$ such that $\vec{v}_{\sigma,\tau}$ is the unique solution to the equation $\vec{v}_{\sigma,\tau} = Q\vec{v}_{\sigma,\tau} + \bar{b}$. Also $I - Q$ is invertible, all entries of $(I - Q)^{-1}$ are non-negative and the entries along the diagonal are strictly positive.*

**Proof:** Substituting 0 for $v_{\sigma,\tau}(i)$, $k + 1 \leq i \leq N - 1$ and 1 for $v_{\sigma,\tau}(N)$ in equations (4.1) and rearranging the terms in the equations, it follows that

$$\vec{v}_{\sigma,\tau} = Q\vec{v}_{\sigma,\tau} + \bar{b},$$

where $\bar{b}$ is a constant vector and $Q$ is the the 1-step transition matrix of the nodes $\{1, \ldots, k\}$. For each $i$, the $i$th component of $\bar{b}$ is from the set $\{0, 1/2, 1\}$ and equals the probability of reaching the accepting node from $i$ in 1 step. Also all entries of $Q$ are in $\{0, 1/2, 1\}$. The equation $\vec{v}_{\sigma,\tau} = Q\vec{v}_{\sigma,\tau} + \bar{b}$ has a unique solution if and only if $(I - Q)$ is invertible.

To prove this, we first argue that $\lim_{n \to \infty} Q^n = 0$. Note that any random walk from a node in the set $\{1, \ldots, k\}$ eventually leaves this set since all nodes in this set have a path to a halting node. Since $Q^n$ is the $n$-step transition matrix for the nodes $1, \ldots, k$, it follows that $\lim_{n \to \infty} Q^n = 0$. Kemeny and Snell [23] give a simple argument that uses this fact to show that $I - Q$ is invertible. From simple rules of algebra,

$$I - Q^n = (I - Q)(I + Q + Q^2 + \ldots + Q^{n-1});$$

taking the limit of both sides as $n \to \infty$ yields $I = (I - Q)(I + Q + \ldots + Q^n + \ldots)$. Since the left side has determinant 1, the determinant of the right side must also be 1, implying that $I - Q$ has non-zero determinant. Hence $I - Q$ is invertible. Also, $(I - Q)^{-1} = I + Q + Q^2 + \ldots$; hence every entry of $(I - Q)^{-1}$ is non-negative and the entries along the diagonal are strictly positive. $\square$

The value $v_{\sigma,\tau}(i)$ of each node of the graph $G_{\sigma,\tau}$ has a natural interpretation with respect to game automaton $M$. Suppose $M$ is in the configuration that labels node $i$. Suppose player 1 of $M$ uses the strategy corresponding to existential policy $\sigma$ and that player 0 of $M$ uses the strategy corresponding to universal policy $\tau$ in subsequent moves of the game. Then $v_{\sigma,\tau}(i)$ is the probability that $M$ reaches an accepting state on input $x$. Equivalently, if $\eta_i$ is any node of $T_{\sigma,\tau}$ which is labeled with the same configuration as node $i$ of $G$, then $v_{\sigma,\tau}(i) = value_{\sigma,\tau}(\eta_i)$. We prove this in the following claim.

**Claim 4.2** *If $\eta_i$ is a node of $T_{\sigma,\tau}$ which is labeled with the same configuration as node $i$ of $G$, then*

$$v_{\sigma,\tau}(i) = value_{\sigma,\tau}(\eta_i) \, .$$

**Proof:** If $\eta_i$ is an accepting node then $value_{\sigma,\tau}(\eta_i) = 1 = v_{\sigma,\tau}(i)$. Similarly if $\eta_i$ is a rejecting node, $value_{\sigma,\tau}(\eta_i) = 0 = v_{\sigma,\tau}(i)$. If no node in the subtree of $T_{\sigma,\tau}$ rooted at $\eta_i$ is an accepting node then also node $i$ of graph $G_{\sigma,\tau}$ has no path to an accepting node and again $value_{\sigma,\tau}(\eta_i) = 0 = v_{\sigma,\tau}(i)$.

It remains to consider nodes $\eta_i$ such that some node in a subtree of $T_{\sigma,\tau}$ is an accepting node. Let these nodes be $\{\eta_1, \eta_2, \ldots, \eta_k\}$. From Lemma 4.1, the values of the corresponding nodes $\{1, \ldots, k\}$ of $G$ are the unique solution to the equations (4.1). We show that the values $\{value_{\sigma,\tau}(\eta_i)\}$ are also a solution to these equations.

First consider the case when $\eta_i$ is a coin-tossing node with children $\eta_j$ and $\eta_m$. The labels of nodes $\eta_j$ and $\eta_m$ are the same as the labels of nodes $j$ and $m$ of graph $G_{\sigma,\tau}$. By definition of $value_{\sigma,\tau}(\eta_i)$,

$$value_{\sigma,\tau}(\eta_i) = \lim_{l \to \infty} 1/2[value_{\sigma,\tau}(\eta_j, l) + value_{\sigma,\tau}(\eta_m, l)]$$

$$= 1/2[\lim_{l \to \infty} value_{\sigma,\tau}(\eta_j, l) + \lim_{l \to \infty} value_{\sigma,\tau}(\eta_m, l)]$$

$$= 1/2[value_{\sigma,\tau}(\eta_j) + value_{\sigma,\tau}(\eta_m)] \, .$$

The cases when $\eta_i$ is an existential node or a universal node are similar. Hence the values $\{value_{\sigma,\tau}(\eta_i)\}$ are a solution to the equations (4.1). Since the equations have a unique solution, $value_{\sigma,\tau}(\eta_i) = v_{\sigma,\tau}(i)$, as required. □

In the next claim we relate the value $v_\sigma$ of the computation tree $T_\sigma$ to the values $v_{\sigma,\tau}(start(G_{\sigma,\tau}))$.

**Claim 4.3** *Let $G$ be the graph representation of game automaton $M$ on input $x$. Let $\sigma$ be an existential policy of $G$ corresponding to strategy $\sigma$ of player 1 of $M$ on $x$. Then*
$$v_\sigma = \min_\tau\{v_{\sigma,\tau}(start(G_{\sigma,\tau}))\} .$$

**Proof:**

$$
\begin{aligned}
v_\sigma &= \inf_\tau\{v_{\sigma,\tau}\}, \quad \text{from Lemma 2.4,} \\
&= \inf_\tau\{value_{\sigma,\tau}(root(T_{\sigma,\tau}))\}, \quad \text{by definition of } v_{\sigma,\tau}, \\
&= \inf_\tau\{v_{\sigma,\tau}(start(G_{\sigma,\tau}))\}, \quad \text{from Claim 4.2,} \\
&= \min_\tau\{v_{\sigma,\tau}(start(G_{\sigma,\tau}))\}, \quad \text{since there are finitely many policies } \tau,
\end{aligned}
$$

as required. □

Consider the case when $M$ is a space bounded game automaton in the class $UC$. Then the graph $G$ on input $x$ has no universal nodes and so $G$ has no universal policies. In this case, if $\sigma$ is an existential policy of $G$, we denote by $G_\sigma$ the subgraph $G$ where the edges from the existential nodes are from policy $\sigma$ and we denote the value of node $i$ of $G_\sigma$ by $v_\sigma(i)$. Suppose $M$ is in the configuration that labels node $i$. Suppose player 1 of $M$ uses the strategy corresponding to existential policy $\sigma$ in subsequent moves of the game. Then $v_\sigma(i)$ is the probability that $M$ reaches an accepting state on input $x$. The value of $T_\sigma$ is $v_\sigma = v_\sigma(start(G_\sigma))$. Since there are a finite number of policies of $G$, $x$ is accepted by $M$ if and only if $\max_\sigma\{v_\sigma(start(G_\sigma))\} > 1/2$.

## 4.2   The Halting Property

We mentioned in the introduction to this chapter that a property of space bounded game automata that makes them hard to analyze is the fact that they do not necessarily always halt, even on inputs they accept. In this section we prove that any space bounded game automaton with complete information can be simulated by another game automaton with the same space bound that halts with probability 1. We say a probabilistic game automaton $M$ halts with probability 1 if for all inputs $x$ and all pairs of strategies $\sigma$ and $\tau$ of the players on $x$, the probability of reaching either the accepting or rejecting state on $x$ $x$ when the players use strategies $\sigma$ and $\tau$ is 1. This is proved in Lemma 4.5. We first prove an interesting property of game automata with complete information and space bound $s(n)$: even though the error probability of these game automata is not bounded away from $\frac{1}{2}$, we can show that the error probability must be bounded away from $\frac{1}{2}$ by at least $2^{-c^{s(n)}}$ for some constant $c$. This result is an extension of a result of Gill ([17], Lemma 6.6).

**Lemma 4.4** *Let $M$ be an $s(n)$ space bounded game automaton in the class $\forall UC$. Then there is a constant $c$ such that for every input $x$ and Markov strategy $\sigma$ of $M$ on $x$, the value $v_\sigma$ of the computation tree $T_\sigma$ of $M$ on $x$ satisfies*

$$
\begin{array}{ll}
(i) & \text{if } v_\sigma > \frac{1}{2} \text{ then } v_\sigma > \frac{1}{2} + 2^{-c^{s(|x|)}}, \\
(ii) & \text{if } v_\sigma < \frac{1}{2} \text{ then } v_\sigma < \frac{1}{2} - 2^{-c^{s(|x|)}}.
\end{array}
$$

**Proof:** Let $G$ be the graph which represents $M$ on input $x$ of length $n$. Let $d^{s(n)}$ be the number of nodes of $G$ where $d$ is a constant. To prove $(i)$, suppose $v_\sigma > \frac{1}{2}$. We will show that for any strategy $\tau$ of player 0, the probability $M$ reaches an accepting state is at least $\frac{1}{2} + 2^{-(2d)^{s(n)}}$. Equivalently, we need to show that the value of the start node of $G_{\sigma,\tau}$ is at least $\frac{1}{2} + 2^{-(2d)^{s(n)}}$. The proof that this is so is exactly as in Gill ([17], Lemma 6.6). Let $\{1, 2, \ldots k\}$ be the set of nodes that are not halting and have a path to a halting node. Let $\vec{v}_{\sigma,\tau}$ be the vector $(v_{\sigma,\tau}(\eta_1), v_{\sigma,\tau}(\eta_2) \ldots v_{\sigma,\tau}(\eta_k))^T$. From Lemma 4.1, $\vec{v}_{\sigma,\tau}$ is the unique solution to the equation $(I - Q)\vec{v}_{\sigma,\tau} = \vec{b}$, where $\vec{b}$ is a constant vector and $I - Q$ is a matrix with non-zero determinant. Furthermore the entries in $I - Q$ and $\vec{b}$ are from the set $\{0, \pm\frac{1}{2}, \pm 1\}$. If we multiply both sides of this equation by 2, we have $2(I - Q)\vec{v}_{\sigma,\tau} = 2\vec{b}$, where the entries in $2(I - Q)$ and $2\vec{b}$ are from the set $\{0, \pm 1, \pm 2\}$. By Cramer's rule, the value of node $i \in \{1, 2, \ldots, k\}$ can be represented as $N_i/D$ where $D$ is the determinant of $2(I - Q)$. The determinant of $2(I - Q)$ is at most $4^{d^{s(n)}}$. This follows from expansion by minors, the fact that the entries of $2(I - Q)$ are from the set

$\{0, \pm 1, \pm 2\}$ and that each row has a constant number of non-zero entries, the sum of whose absolute values is at most 4. Thus the value of the start node of $G_{\sigma,\tau}$, $v_{\sigma,\tau}(start(G_{\sigma,\tau}))$, is the quotient of two numbers of value at most $4^{d^{s(n)}}$. Furthermore, $v_{\sigma,\tau}(start(G_{\sigma,\tau})) > \frac{1}{2}$ and hence has value at least $\frac{1}{2} + 2^{-(2d)^{s(n)}}$. Let $c = 2d$. Since from Lemma 4.3, $v_{\sigma} = \min_{\tau}\{v_{\sigma,\tau}(start(G_{\sigma,\tau}))\}$ it follows that $v_{\sigma} > \frac{1}{2} + 2^{-c^{s(n)}}$, as required. Note that the constant $c$ here is independent of $\sigma$, $\tau$ and $x$. The proof of $(ii)$ is similar. $\square$

Next we show that any $s(n)$ space bounded game automaton in the class $\forall UC$ can be simulated by an $s(n)$ space bounded game automaton in the same class that halts with probability 1 and runs in expected time $2^{2^{O(s(n))}}$.

**Lemma 4.5** *Let $s(n)$ be space constructible and let $M$ be a $s(n)$ space bounded game automaton from the class $\forall UC$ (UC, BC or $\forall BC$). Then there is an $s(n)$ space bounded game automaton $M'$ from the class $\forall UC$ (UC, BC or $\forall BC$, respectively) that accepts the same language as $M$, halts with probability 1 and runs in expected time $2^{2^{O(s(n))}}$ on any strategies of the players of $M'$.*

**Proof:** The proof is very similar to a proof of Ruzzo, Simon and Tompa [31]. They show that if $M$ is a probabilistic $s(n)$ space-bounded Turing machine, then $M$ can be simulated by a probabilistic $s(n)$ space-bounded Turing machine $M'$ which halts on all inputs with probability 1 and runs in expected time at most $2^{2^{O(s(n))}}$. With very little modification, the proof extends to space-bounded game automata with complete information. First consider the case when $M$ is an $s(n)$ space bounded game automaton in the class $\forall UC$. Let $c$ be the constant from Lemma 4.4. Let $d$ be a constant such that the number of configurations of $M$ on inputs of length $n$ is at most $d^{s(n)}$. On input $x$ of length $n$, $M'$ executes the algorithm of Figure 4.1.

To simulate $M$, player $1'$ of $M'$ simulates the steps of player 1 of $M$ and player $0'$ simulates the steps of player 0. Player 0 can write down $(c + d)^{s(n)}$ since this number is of length $s(n)$ and $s(n)$ is space constructible. Clearly $M'$ can execute the algorithm in $O(s(n))$ space. Also $M'$ halts with probability 1 since the probability that $M'$ reaches the $i$th round of the repeat loop is $(1 - 2^{-(c+d)^{s(n)}})^{i-1} \to 0$ as $i \to \infty$. The expected running time of $M'$ is at most $2^{(c+d)^{s(n)}}$ since the probability that all coin tosses of a round are tails is $2^{-(c+d)^{s(n)}}$. If $M$ rejects $x$ then $M'$ also rejects $x$ because the probability that

> repeat
> 
> > simulate $M$ on $x$ for $d^{s(n)}$ further steps;
> > if $M$ enters an accepting state at any step then
> > > halt in an accepting state;
> > 
> > Player 0: toss $(c+d)^{s(n)}$ coins;
> > if all are tails then
> > > halt in a rejecting state.
> 
> endrepeat

Figure 4.1: *Simulation of $s(n)$ space bounded game automata $M$ by $M'$ that halts with probability 1, Lemma 4.4.*

$M'$ accepts any input is at most the probability $M$ accepts the input. Finally we need to show that if $M$ accepts $x$ then so does $M'$. Let $\sigma$ be a winning strategy of player 1 of $M$ on $x$, and let $\tau$ be the best possible strategy of player 0 against strategy $\sigma$. If the players of $M'$ use strategies $\sigma$ and $\tau$ when simulating $M$ then the probability that $M'$ accepts $x$ is at least

$$v_\sigma - \sum_{i=1}^{\infty} (\quad \text{Prob}[\ ith \text{ round of the repeat loop is reached}] \times$$
$$\text{Prob}[\text{ all cointosses of } ith \text{ round are tails}] \times$$
$$\text{Prob}[M' \text{ halts after the } ith \text{ round given that}$$
$$M' \text{ reaches an accepting state}]\quad).$$

We claim that the probability $M'$ halts after the $ith$ round, given that $M'$ reaches an accepting state on $x$, is at most $(1 - 2^{-d^{s(n)}})^i$. Consider the subgraph of $G_{\sigma,\tau}$ consisting of all nodes with a path to the node labeled by the accepting configuration. On any computation in which $M'$ eventually reaches an accepting state on $x$, at the start of each round of the repeat loop $M$ must be in a configuration labeling a node of this subgraph. The node labeled by an accepting configuration is reachable from any other node in the subgraph within $d^{s(n)}$ steps and hence with probability at least $2^{-d^{s(n)}}$. Therefore an accepting configuration must be reachable with probability $\geq 2^{-d^{s(n)}}$ from the configuration at the start of every round of the repeat loop and so the probability that $M$ fails to accept for $i$ iterations is at most $(1 - 2^{-d^{s(n)}})^i$. Hence the probability that $M'$ accepts $x$ is at least

$$v_\sigma - \sum_{i=1}^{\infty}(1 - 2^{-(c+d)s(n)})^{i-1} \; 2^{-(c+d)s(n)} \; (1 - 2^{-ds(n)})^i$$
$$\geq \; v_\sigma - 2^{-(c+d)s(n)}\sum_{i=1}^{\infty}(1 - 2^{-ds(n)})^i$$
$$\geq \; v_\sigma - 2^{-(c+d)s(n)} \; 2^{ds(n)}$$
$$\geq \; v_\sigma - 2^{-cs(n)} \; .$$

If $\sigma$ is a winning strategy of $M$ on $x$ then $v_\sigma - 2^{-cs(n)} > \frac{1}{2}$, by Lemma 4.4, and so $M'$ accepts $x$. This completes the proof in the case when $M$ is in the class $\forall UC$. The proof is identical when $M$ is in the class $UC$, since $UC$ is a subclass of $\forall UC$. When $M$ is in the classes $\forall BC$ or $BC$ then for any bounded random winning strategy $\sigma$ of $M$, $v_\sigma$ is bounded above $\frac{1}{2}$ by a constant and thus also $v_\sigma - 2^{-cs(n)}$ is bounded above $\frac{1}{2}$ by a constant for sufficiently large $c$. Hence $M'$ is also a bounded random game automaton accepting the same language as $M$. $\square$

## 4.3    Arthur-Merlin Games

We can now prove the first part of the main result of this chapter, that any language recognized by an $s(n)$ space bounded alternating Turing machine can be recognized by an $s(n)$ space bounded Arthur-Merlin game. A related result was proved by Ruzzo, Simon and Tompa [31]: they showed that $\Sigma_k-ASPACE(s(n)) \subseteq BSPACE(s(n))$ for all constants $k$. Here $\Sigma_k-ASPACE(s(n))$ is the class of languages accepted by alternating Turing machines with space bound $s(n)$ which have at most $k$ alternations between the players, and $BSPACE(s(n))$ is the class of languages accepted by probabilistic Turing machines with space bound $s(n)$ and error probability bounded away from $1/2$.

**Theorem 4.6** *For space constructible* $s(n)$,

$$ASPACE(s(n)) \subseteq BC\text{--}SPACE(s(n)) \; .$$

**Proof:** Let $M$ be an $s(n)$ space bounded game automaton in the class $\forall C$. Let $d^{s(n)}$ be an upper bound on the number of possible configurations of

$M$ on an input of length $n$, where $d$ is a constant. Without loss of generality we can assume that the computation tree of $M$ on any input of length $n$ is a complete tree with depth exactly $d^{s(n)}$, and that the players of $M$ alternate turns at every step. We define an automaton $M'$ which recognizes the same language as $M$. The idea is that on any input $x$, $M'$ simulates $M$ many times on $x$. If $M$ reaches an accepting state on all of the simulations, $M'$ accepts $x$; otherwise $M'$ rejects $x$. The number of times $M'$ simulates $M$ has expected value $2^{(d^{s(|x|)}+3)}$. Figure 4.2 describes the algorithm of the players of $M'$ on input $x$.

> repeat
>         simulate $M$ on $x$ until a halting state is reached;
>         if a rejecting state of $M$ is reached then
>             halt in a rejecting state
>         else
>             toss $d^{s(|x|)} + 3$ coins;
>             if all are tails then halt and accept
> endrepeat

Figure 4.2: *Simulation of an alternating Turing machine $M$ by an Arthur-Merlin game $M'$ with the same space bound, Theorem 4.6.*

Since $M$ is bounded by space $s(n)$, the simulations of $M$ by $M'$ at each iteration of the loop can be done simply by letting player $0'$ simulate the steps of player 0 and player $1'$ simulate the steps of player 1. Hence $M'$ is also $s(n)$ space bounded. However player $0'$ cannot make universal moves; hence to simulate a universal move of player 0 it randomly chooses one of the possible moves of player 0.

Player 0 can write down $d^{s(n)}$ since this number has length $s(n)$ and $s(n)$ is space constructible. Thus clearly $M'$ can execute the algorithm in $O(s(n))$ space. It is also not hard to see that if $M$ accepts $x$ then player $1'$ of $M'$ has a bounded winning strategy on $x$ — in fact, player $1'$ has a strategy which has value 1. Finally we need to show that if $M$ rejects $x$ then so does $M'$. It is straightforward to see that the probability that $M'$ reaches an accepting state on $x$ is at most

$$\sum_{i=1}^{\infty}(\quad \text{Prob}[\ ith \text{ round of the repeat loop is reached}]\times$$

$$\text{Prob}[\text{ all cointosses of } ith \text{ round are tails}]\times$$

$$\text{Prob}[M' \text{ does not reach a rejecting state in } i \text{ simulations of } M\ ]\ ).$$

The probability that all coin tosses of a round are tails is $2^{-(d^{s(n)}+3)}$; thus the probability that $M'$ reaches the $ith$ round of the repeat loop is at most $(1 - 2^{-(d^{s(n)}+3)})^{i-1}$. Suppose that on some fixed iteration of the repeat loop, player $1'$ simulates a strategy $\sigma$ of the existential player of $M$ on $x$. The probability that $M'$ reaches a rejecting state on a simulation of $M$ is at least $2^{-d^{s(n)}}$. To see this, note that the running time of $M$ is bounded by $d^{s(n)}$; hence the computation tree $T_\sigma$ of $M$ corresponding to strategy $\sigma$ has at most $2^{(d^{s(n)})}$ leaves. Each time the players of $M'$ simulate $M$, they follow a random path of tree $T_\sigma$. Thus each leaf of $T_\sigma$ is reached with equal probability. Since $M$ rejects $x$, one of these leaves must be rejecting; hence on one round of a simulation of $M$ a rejecting state is reached with probability at least $2^{-d^{s(n)}}$. Since this is true on every round of the simulation, regardless of what strategy player $1'$ uses, the probability that $M$ does not reach a rejecting state of $M$ after $i$ simulations of $M$ is at most $(1 - 2^{-d^{s(n)}})^i$. Combining these expressions, we see that the probability that $M'$ accepts $x$ is at most

$$\sum_{i=1}^{\infty}(1 - 2^{-(d^{s(n)}+3)})^{i-1} \cdot 2^{-(d^{s(n)}+3)} \cdot \left(1 - 2^{-d^{s(n)}}\right)^i$$

$$\leq\ 2^{-(d^{s(n)}+3)}\sum_{i=1}^{\infty}(1 - 2^{-d^{s(n)}})^i$$

$$\leq\ 2^{-(d^{s(n)}+3)} \cdot 2^{d^{s(n)}}$$

$$\leq\ 2^{-3}\ <\ \tfrac{1}{4}.$$

Hence $M'$ is also a bounded random game automaton accepting the same language as $M$. In fact, it is interesting to note that $M'$ is a one-sided error game automaton, that is, $M'$ halts in a rejecting state with probability 0 on inputs accepted by $M$. $\square$

# 4.4   Games Against Nature

The goal of this section is to show that any language accepted by a game against nature with space bound $s(n)$ can be recognized by a deterministic Turing machine which runs in time $k^{s(n)}$ for some constant $k$. Equivalently, we will show that $UC\text{--}SPACE(s(n)) \subseteq \cup_{c>0}DTIME(2^{cs(n)})$. It turns out that the graphs associated with space bounded game automata with complete information can be interpreted as special kinds of Markov decision processes [21]. We start this section by defining a Markov decision process (we assume the reader is familiar with the definition of a Markov process, but not necessarily with the definition of a Markov decision process). We show how the class of space bounded game automata in the class $UC$ is related to Markov decision processes, and describe some simple properties of Markov decision processes. These properties will be used in our main result.

## 4.4.1   Markov Decision Processes

A thorough treatment of finite state Markov decision processes is given by Howard [21]; our definition here is less general than that considered by Howard. A finite state *Markov decision process* $\mathcal{G}$ consists of a set of states $\{1, \ldots, N\}$ where each state $i$ has a finite set of *choices* $E_i$. Each choice $p_i \in E_i$ is a vector $(p_{i1}, \ldots, p_{iN})$ where $\sum_j p_{ij} = 1$. State 1 is called the *start* state, state $N-1$ is the 0-sink state and state $N$ is the 1-sink state. We assume that for all $p_{N-1} \in E_{N-1}, p_{N-1,i} = 0$ for $i \neq N-1$. Similarly, for all $p_N \in E_N, p_{N,i} = 0$ for $i \neq N$.

We define a *policy* $P$ of $\mathcal{G}$ to be a matrix $P = [p_{ij}]$ $1 \leq i \leq N$ where for all $i$, row $i$ of $P$ is a choice of $E_i$. The states $\{1, \ldots, N\}$ together with policy $P$ form a Markov process where $p_{ij}$ is the probability of going from state $i$ to state $j$ in one step. We denote this Markov process by $\mathcal{G}_P$. We will assume in this section that the $p_{ij}$ can be written as the quotient of two integers which have binary representation of length at most $N$. This assumption is general enough for our purposes, and implies that the decision process can be represented in binary by a string of length polynomial in $N$.

For any policy $P$, we associate a value $v_P(i)$ with each node $i$ of Markov decision process $\mathcal{G}$ as follows. For a policy $P$, let the values of the states of $\mathcal{G}$, denoted by $\{v_P(i), i = 1, \ldots, N\}$, be the unique values satisfying the following conditions.

$$v_P(N-1) = 0,$$
$$v_P(N) = 1,$$
$$v_P(i) = \begin{cases} 0, & \text{if the probability of reaching a sink state from state } i \text{ is } 0 \\ \sum_{j=1}^{N} p_{ij} v_P(j), & \text{otherwise.} \end{cases}$$

**Lemma 4.7** *The values $v_P(i)$ of $\mathcal{G}$ are well defined and can be evaluated in time polynomial in $N$.*

**Proof:** The proof that the values are well-defined is exactly like the proof of Lemma 4.1 that the values of the subgraph $G_{\sigma,\tau}$ are well defined. It is clearly true for values $v_P(i)$ when the probability of reaching a sink state from state $i$ is 0, since then $v_P(i) = 0$. Also the values of the sink states $N-1$ and $N$ can easily be seen to be well-defined. Let states $1, \ldots, k$ be the states from which the probability of reaching a sink state is greater than zero. Let $\vec{v}_P = (v_P(1), \ldots, v_P(k))^T$. Then just as in Lemma 4.1, $\vec{v}_P = Q\vec{v}_P + \vec{b}$, where $\vec{b}$ is a constant vector, $Q$ is the one-step transition matrix of states $1, \ldots, k$ of $\mathcal{G}$ with respect to $P$ and $I - Q$ is invertible. The values $v_P(i)$ can be computed in time polynomial in $N$ by solving the equation $\vec{v}_P = Q\vec{v}_P + \vec{b}$ using any standard method, for example Cramer's rule [3]. Note that because of our assumption on the representation of the $p_{ij}$, the entries of the matrix $Q$ can be represented as the quotient of integers of length at most $N$, and thus Cramer's rule can be applied in time polynomial in $N$. $\square$

If $M$ is an $s(n)$ space bounded game automaton in the class $UC$, the graph $G$ associated with $M$ on input $x$ corresponds to a special kind of Markov decision process. The nodes of $G$ are the states of the Markov decision process. We let $\mathcal{G}$ denote the Markov decision process corresponding to graph $G$. The start state of $\mathcal{G}$ is the start node of $G$ and the 0- and 1-sink states are the rejecting and accepting nodes, respectively. If $i$ is an existential node of $G$ then state $i$ of $\mathcal{G}$ has two choices, each of the form $p_i = (0, \ldots, 0, 1, 0, \ldots, 0)$ where the $j$th entry of $p_i$ is 1 if $(i, j)$ is an outgoing edge of node $i$ and all other entries of $p_i$ are 0. If $i$ is a coin-tossing node of $G$, state $i$ of $\mathcal{G}$ has one choice of the form $p_i = (0, \ldots, 0, \frac{1}{2}, 0, \ldots, 0, \frac{1}{2}, 0, \ldots, 0)$ where the $j$th and $k$th entries of $p_i$ are $\frac{1}{2}$ if $(i, j), (i, k)$ are the outgoing edges of node $i$ and all other entries of $p_i$ are 0. Each existential policy $\sigma$ of $G$ corresponds to a policy $P$ of the Markov decision process in a natural way. The definitions of the values of the nodes of graph $G$ with respect to policy $\sigma$ are consistent with the definitions of the values of the states of the Markov decision process $\mathcal{G}$ with respect to policy $P$.

**Lemma 4.8** *If $\mathcal{G}$ is a Markov decision process corresponding to a probabilistic game automaton $M$ on $x$ where $M$ halts with probability 1 on $x$, then the equations*

$$v_P(N-1) = 0,$$
$$v_P(N) = 1,$$
$$v_P(i) = \sum_{j=1}^{N} p_{ij} v_P(j), \text{ for } 1 \le i \le N-2$$

*have a unique solution.*

**Proof:** If $M$ halts with probability 1 on $x$ then in the corresponding Markov decision process $\mathcal{G}$, all states have a path to a sink state. Then from Lemma 4.7, the above equations have a unique solution. $\square$

## 4.4.2 Main Theorem

We can now outline the proof the second of our main results in this chapter, that $UC\text{--}SPACE(s(n)) \subseteq \cup_{c \ge 0} DTIME(2^{cs(n)})$. Let $L$ be a language in the class $UC\text{--}SPACE(s(n))$ and let $M$ be an $s(n)$ space bounded game automaton in the class $UC$ that accepts $L$. From Lemma 4.5, we can assume without loss of generality that $M$ halts with probability 1 on evey input. Let $G$ be the graph representation of $M$ on input $x$ and let $\mathcal{G}$ be the Markov decision process corresponding to graph $G$. We have already seen at the end of Section 4.1 that $x$ is accepted by $M$ if and only if

$$\max_{\sigma}\{v_\sigma(start(G))\} > \frac{1}{2},$$

where the maximum is taken over all policies $\sigma$ of graph $G$. Equivalently, $x$ is accepted by $M$ if and only if

$$\max_{P}\{v_P(start(\mathcal{G}))\} > \frac{1}{2},$$

where the maximum here is taken over all policies $P$ of $\mathcal{G}$ and $start(\mathcal{G})$ denotes the start state of G. This is because of the correspondence between policies of graph $G$ and the policies of the Markov decision process $\mathcal{G}$. We say a policy $P$ of $\mathcal{G}$ is *optimal* if $v_P(start(\mathcal{G})) \geq v_{P'}(start(\mathcal{G}))$ for all policies $P'$ of $\mathcal{G}$. An optimal policy always exists since the number of policies is finite. Thus the value of the start state of $\mathcal{G}$, with respect to an optimal policy, is greater than $\frac{1}{2}$ if and only if $M$ accepts $x$. To prove the theorem, we use results on Markov decision processes that show how the values of the states of $\mathcal{G}$ with respect to an optimal policy can be computed in time polynomial in the number of states of $\mathcal{G}$, by a reduction to linear programming. We include all the necessary results here for completeness and because we can simplify the proof for the special type of Markov decision process which we have defined here.

The proof can be broken down into two major steps. First we show that the values $v_{opt}(i)$ of the states of $\mathcal{G}$ with respect to some optimal policy are the unique solution to the following equations:

$$
v_{opt}(i) = \begin{cases}
\max\limits_{p_i \in E_i} \sum\limits_{j=1}^{N} p_{ij} v_{opt}(j), & \text{if } 1 \leq i \leq N - 2, \\
0, & \text{if } i = N - 1, \\
1, & \text{if } i = N.
\end{cases}
\tag{4.2}
$$

The breakdown of this step is as follows. In Lemma 4.9 we show that the values of the states of $\mathcal{G}$, with respect to *some* policy, satisfy Equations (4.2). Lemma 4.11 is a technical lemma, from which we derive in Lemma 4.12 that Equations (4.2) have a unique solution, completing the first major step of the proof. The second major step is to show that the unique solution of Equations (4.2) can be found in time polynomial in $N$, the number of states of $\mathcal{G}$. This is shown in Lemma 4.13. Theorem 4.14 combines the results of all of these lemmas to get the final result.

**Lemma 4.9** *There is a policy $P^{(opt)}$ of $\mathcal{G}$ such that the values $\{v_{opt}(i)\}$ of the states of $\mathcal{G}$ with respect to $P^{(opt)}$ satisfy Equations (4.2).*

**Proof:**    We give an algorithm in Figure 4.3 to construct $P^{(opt)}$. This algorithm, called the *Policy Iteration Algorithm*, is due to Howard [21]. Unfortunately the algorithm may run in time exponential in the number of states of $\mathcal{G}$. The algorithm proceeds in iterations. There is a *current* policy for each iteration and the current policy for the initial iteration is chosen arbitrarily.

At each iteration the algorithm modifies the current policy in a special way to obtain a new policy which becomes the current policy of the next iteration. The algorithm stops when the current policy satisfies Equations (4.2). Let the policy $P^{(opt)}$ be the current policy of the last iteration of the algorithm and let $v_{opt}(i)$ be the values of $\mathcal{G}$ with respect to policy $P^{(opt)}$. The algorithm is given in Figure 4.3.

Let $P'$ be an arbitrary policy of $\mathcal{G}$.
repeat
$\quad\overline{P \leftarrow P'};$
$\quad$compute $v_P(i)$ for $1 \leq i \leq N$;
$\quad\underline{\text{if}}$ $v_P(i)$ satisfies Equations (4.2) for each $i$ $\underline{\text{then}}$
$\quad\quad$halt and let $P^{(opt)} = P$;
$\quad\underline{\text{else}}$
$\quad\quad$let $i$ be such that $v_P(i) < \max_{p_i \in E_i} \sum_j p_{ij} v_P(j)$;
$\quad\quad$let $p'_i = (p'_{i1}, \ldots, p'_{iN}) \in E_i$ be such that $\sum p'_{ij} v_P(j) > v_P(i)$;
$\quad\quad$let $p'_k = p_k$, for $k \neq i$;
$\quad\quad$let $P' = [p'_{ij}]$.
endrepeat

Figure 4.3: *Policy iteration algorithm (Howard).*

It follows from Lemma 4.7, the $v_P(i)$ can be computed in time polynomial in $N$ at each iteration, since the probabilities $p_{ij}$ are all from the set $\{0, 1/2, 1\}$. Thus it is straightforward to show that each iteration can be completed in time polynomial in $N$. Clearly if the algorithm halts, it outputs a policy whose values satisfy Equations (4.2). Hence we need only show that the algorithm always halts. To do this we need the following claim.

**Claim 4.10** *If $P'$ is the policy obtained from policy $P$ on some iteration of the algorithm then for all $l$, $v_{P'}(l) \geq v_P(l)$ and $\sum_l v_{P'}(l) > \sum_l v_P(l)$.*

**Proof:** If $v_P(l) = 0$ then trivially $v_{P'}(l) \geq v_P(l)$. Hence we only consider $l$ such that $v_P(l) > 0$. We first show that if $v_P(l) > 0$ then $v_{P'}(l) > 0$. To do this we consider the graph representation of the Markov processes $\mathcal{G}_P$ and $\mathcal{G}_{P'}$, where each state is represented by a node and there is an edge between node $i$ and node $j$ labeled $p_{ij}$ in $G_P$, $p'_{ij}$ in $G_{P'}$ if there is a positive probability of reaching state $j$ from state $i$ in Markov process $\mathcal{G}_P$ and $\mathcal{G}_{P'}$, respectively. To show that if $v_P(l) > 0$ then $v_{P'}(l) > 0$, it is sufficient to show that if there is a path from $l$ to $N$ in the graph representing $\mathcal{G}_P$ then there is a path from $l$ to $N$ in the graph representing $\mathcal{G}_{P'}$. First suppose that there is a path from $l$ to $N$ in the graph representing $\mathcal{G}_P$ that does not go through node $i$. Then the same path exists in the graph representing $\mathcal{G}_{P'}$, since the only difference between the graphs representing $\mathcal{G}_P$ and $\mathcal{G}_{P'}$ is in the outgoing edges of node $i$. If the path from $l$ to $N$ in the graph representing $\mathcal{G}_P$ does go through $i$, then there is also a path from $l$ to $N$, which goes through $i$, in the graph representing $\mathcal{G}_{P'}$. To see this, note that there is a path from $l$ to $i$ in $\mathcal{G}_{P'}$ if there is in $\mathcal{G}_P$. Also since $v_{P'}(i) > v_P(i) \geq 0$, there is a path from $i$ to $N$ in $\mathcal{G}_{P'}$. Thus if $v_P(l) > 0$ then $v_{P'}(l) > 0$.

Without loss of generality assume that the nodes of $\mathcal{G}_{P'}$ which have value greater than 0 are numbered $1, \ldots, k$. For $l \in \{1, \ldots, k\}$, let $\Delta_l = v_{P'}(l) - v_P(l)$. Then $\Delta_l = \sum_{j=1}^{k} p'_{lj} v_{P'}(j) - \sum_{j=1}^{k} p_{lj} v_P(j)$. Adding and subtracting $\sum_{j=1}^{k} p'_{lj} v_P(j)$ we obtain

$$\Delta_l = \sum_{j=1}^{k} p'_{lj} v_{P'}(j) - \sum_{j-1}^{k} p'_{lj} v_P(j) + \sum_{j=1}^{k} p'_{lj} v_P(j) - \sum_{j=1}^{k} p_{lj} v_P(j).$$

Let $\delta_l = \sum_{j=1}^{k} p'_{lj} v_P(j) - \sum_{j=1}^{k} p_{lj} v_P(j)$. Note that $\delta_i > 0$, by the choice of $P'$, and for $l \neq i$, $\delta_l = 0$. Then

$$\Delta_l = \sum_{j=1}^{k} p'_{lj} \Delta_j + \delta_l.$$

Let $\Delta = (\Delta_1, \ldots, \Delta_k)^T$ and $\delta = (\delta_1, \ldots, \delta_k)^T$. Let $Q'$ be the $k \times k$ submatrix $P'$ such that the $ij$th entry of $Q'$ is the $ij$th entry of $P'$, for $1 \leq i, j \leq k$. Then $\Delta = Q'\Delta + \delta$ which implies that $\Delta = (I - Q')^{-1}\delta$. Since the value $v_{P'}(i) > 0$ for all nodes $i \in 1, \ldots, k$, $I - Q'$ is invertible, just as in Lemma 4.1. In fact, $(I - Q')^{-1} = (Q')^0 + (Q')^1 + \ldots (Q')^n \ldots$. Hence all entries in the vector $(I - Q')^{-1}\delta$ are non-negative. Thus for each $l$, $\Delta_l = v_{P'}(l) - v_P(l)$ is non-negative. Moreover $v_{P'}(i) - v_P(i) > 0$. This is because

$$v_{P'}(i) - v_P(i) = \Delta_i = \sum_{j=1}^{k} p'_{ij}\Delta_j + \delta_i > 0 \; ,$$

since $\delta_i > 0$ and $p'_{ij}$ and $\Delta_j \geq 0$ for $1 \leq j \leq N$. Thus $\sum_l v_{P'}(l) > \sum_l v_P(l)$, completing the proof of the claim. $\square$

It is now straightforward to show that the algorithm halts. From the above claim, the sum of the values of the current policy at each iteration is strictly greater than that of previous iterations. Hence the current policy is never the same on two different iterations. There are at most $2^N$ policies so the algorithm must eventually halt and the number of iterations is bounded by the number of policies. Since each iteration takes time polynomial in $N$, the algorithm runs in worst case time $2^{O(N)}$. $\square$

**Lemma 4.11** *If $\{v_{arb}(i)\}$ are the values of the states of $\mathcal{G}$ with respect to an arbitrary policy $P^{(arb)}$ then for any solution $\{v(i)\}$ of Equations (4.2), $v_{arb}(i) \leq v(i)$ for $1 \leq i \leq N$.*

**Proof:** Clearly $v(N-1) = v_{arb}(N-1) = 0$ and $v(N) = v_{arb}(N) = 1$. Since the game automaton $M$ corresponding to $\mathcal{G}$ halts with probability 1, states $1, \ldots N-2$ of $\mathcal{G}$ have a path to a sink state of $\mathcal{G}$. Let $\vec{v}_{arb} = (v_{arb}(1), \ldots, v_{arb}(N-2))^T$ and let $\vec{v} = (v(1), \ldots, v(N-2))^T$. Then just as in Lemma 4.1, $\vec{v}_{arb} = Q\vec{v}_{arb} + \vec{b}$ where $Q$ is the one-step transition matrix on states $1 \ldots, N-2$ of $\mathcal{G}$ with respect to $P^{(arb)}$ and $\vec{b}$ is a constant vector whose $i$th component is the probability of reaching the accepting state from $i$ in one step in $\mathcal{G}_P$. Furthermore $(I - Q)$ has non-zero determinant; hence $\vec{v}_{arb} = (I - Q)^{-1}\vec{b}$.

Similarly, since the $v(i)$ satisfy Equations (4.2) then $\vec{v} \geq Q\vec{v} + \vec{b}$. Hence $\vec{v} \geq (I - Q)^{-1}\vec{b} = \vec{v}_{arb}$. $\square$

As an immediate corollory of Lemma 4.11 we have:

**Lemma 4.12** *The Equations (4.2) have a unique solution.*

**Proof:**    From Lemma 4.9, it follows that a solution to Equations (4.2) exists. Let $\{v(i)\}$ and $\{v'(i)\}$ be two solutions to Equations (4.2). We show that $v(i) = v'(i), 1 \leq i \leq N$.

We associate policies $P$ with solution $\{v(i)\}$ as follows. For each node $i$, let $p_i \in E_i$ be some choice for which $v(i) = \sum_{j=1}^{N} p_{ij} v(j)$. Such a $p_i$ exists since the $\{v(i)\}$ satisfy Equations (4.2). Let $P$ be the matrix $[p_{ij}]$. Similarly, we associate a policy $P'$ with solution $\{v'(i)\}$. By this definition of $P$ and $P'$ it is immediate that the values $v(i)$ satisfy the equations: $v(i) = 0$, if $i = N - 1$, $v(i) = 1$, if $i = N$ and $v(i) = \sum_{j=1}^{N} p_{ij} v(j)$ otherwise. From Lemma 4.8, these equations have a unique solution and furthermore for $1 \leq i \leq N$, $v(i) = v_P(i)$, the value of node $i$ of $\mathcal{G}$ with respect to policy $P$. In a similar way, it follows that $v'(i) = v_{P'}(i), 1 \leq i \leq N$.

It follows Lemma 4.11 that $v_P(i) \leq v_{P'}(i)$ and $v_{P'}(i) \leq v_P(i)$, proving that $v_P(i) = v_{P'}(i), 1 \leq i \leq N$. Hence $v(i) = v'(i), 1 \leq i \leq N$, as required.    $\square$

**Lemma 4.13** *The unique solution to Equations (4.2) can be found in time polynomial in $N$.*

**Proof:**    Derman [12] showed that the solution to Equations (4.2) can be found by solving the following linear programming problem: minimize $\sum_{i=1}^{N} v(i)$, subject to the constraints

$$v(i) \geq \sum_{j=1}^{N} p_{ij} v(j) \text{ for all } (p_{i1}, \ldots, p_{iN}) \in E_i, 1 \leq i \leq N - 2,$$

$$v(i) \geq 0, 1 \leq i \leq N - 1, \text{ and } v(N) \geq 1 .$$

Let $\{v(i), 1 \leq i \leq N\}$ be an optimal solution to the linear programming problem. A feasible solution exists, for example, the values $v_{opt}(i)$, defined in Lemma 4.9. From the constraints of the linear programming problem it is immediate that

$$v(i) \geq \max_{p_i \in E_i} \sum_{j=1}^{N} p_{ij} v(j), v(N - 1) \geq 0 \text{ and } v(N) \geq 1 .$$

We argue that the $v(i)$ satisfy Equations (4.2) by contradiction. Suppose not; then one of the following must hold: (i) $v(k) > \max_{p_k \in E_k} \sum_{j=1}^{N} p_{kj} v(j)$, for some

$k < N - 1$, (ii) $v(N - 1) > 0$ or (iii) $v(N) > 1$. In each case we construct a vector $\vec{v}' = (v'(1), \ldots v'(N))$ such that $\vec{v}'$ satisfies the constraints of the linear programming problem and $\sum v'(i) < \sum v(i)$, contradicting the fact that values $\{v(i)\}$ are the optimal solution to the linear programming problem. In the first case let $v'(i) = v(i)$ for $i \neq k$ and let $v'(k) = \max_{p_k \in E_k} \sum_{j=1}^{N} p_{kj} v(j)$. In the second case let $v'(N - 1) = 0$ and $v'(i) = v(i)$ for $i \neq N - 1$. Similarly for the third case where $v(N) > 1$, let $v'(N) = 1, v(i)' = v(i)$ for $i \neq N$. In all cases $\{v'(i)\}$ satisfies the constraints of the linear programming problem since for $1 \leq i \leq N - 2$, $v'(i) \geq \sum_{j=1}^{N} p_{ij} v(j) \geq \sum_{j=1}^{N} p_{ij} v'(j)$ for all $(p_{i1}, \ldots, p_{iN}) \in E_i$ and also $v(N - 1) \geq 0$, $v(N) \geq 1$. Also since for some $i, v'(i) < v(i)$, $\sum_{i=1}^{N} v(i)' < \sum_{i=1}^{N} v(i)$, which proves the contradiction. Hence an optimal solution to the linear programming problem must be the unique solution to Equations (4.2). Khachian [24] has shown that the linear programming problem is computable in time polynomial in the length of the input, which is $O(N)$ in this case, since the probabilities $p_{ij}$ are constants. Hence the unique solution of Equations (4.2) can be found in time polynomial in $N$. $\square$

We can finally prove the main theorem of this section.

**Theorem 4.14** *If $s(n) = \Omega(\log n)$ then*

$$UC\text{--}SPACE(s(n)) \subseteq \cup_{c \geq 0} DTIME(2^{cs(n)}).$$

**Proof:** Let $M$ be an $s(n)$ space bounded game automaton in the class $UC$. We describe a $2^{O(s(n))}$ time bounded deterministic Turing machine $M'$ that recognizes the same language as $M$. On input $x$, the game automaton $M'$ constructs the Markov decision process $\mathcal{G}$ corresponding to the graph representing $M$ on $x$. If $s(n)$ is space constructible, this is straightforward; otherwise $M'$ tries $s(n) = 1, 2, \ldots$, until it finds a space bound such that the maximum length of the configurations labeling the nodes of $\mathcal{G}$ is within that bound. Since $s(n) = \Omega(\log n)$, this can be done in time polynomial in $d^{s(n)}$ where $d^{s(n)}$ is the number of distinct configurations of $M$. Let $N = d^{s(n)}$. From Lemmas 4.9 and 4.12, the values of the states of $\mathcal{G}$ with respect to some optimal policy are the unique solution of Equations 4.2. $M'$ finds this solution in time polynomial in $d^{s(n)}$, using the method of Lemma 4.13. $M'$ accepts if and only if the value of the start state of $\mathcal{G}$ is $> \frac{1}{2}$. Hence the total running time is $2^{O(s(n))}$, as required. $\square$

We combine the main results of the chapter in the following theorem.

**Theorem 4.15** *If $s(n) = \Omega(\log n)$ is space constructible, then*

$$BC\text{--}SPACE(s(n)) = UC\text{--}SPACE(s(n)) = ASPACE(s(n)) \ .$$

**Proof:** The result follows immediately from Theorems 4.6 and 4.14. □

It is not known whether Theorem 4.14 can be extended to show that $\forall UC\text{--}SPACE(s(n)) \subseteq ASPACE(s(n))$. It remains an open problem whether this is actually the case. However is straightforward to extend Theorem 4.14 to obtain the following result.

**Theorem 4.16** *For $s(n) = \Omega(\log n)$,*

$$\forall UC\text{--}SPACE(s(n)) \subseteq \cup_c NTIME(2^{cs(n)}) \ .$$

**Proof:** Let $M$ be an $s(n)$ space bounded game automaton in the class $\forall UC$. Without loss of generality we can assume that $M$ halts with probability 1, from Lemma 4.5. We will describe a nondeterministic Turing machine $M'$ that recognizes the same language as $M$. Fix an input $x$. By the definition of language acceptance, $x$ is accepted by $M$ if and only if there exists a strategy $\sigma$ of player 1 of $M$ on $x$ such that $v_\sigma > \frac{1}{2}$. Let $G$ be the graph representation of $M$ on $x$. From Claim 4.3, $x$ is accepted by $M$ if and only if there exists an existential policy $\sigma$ of $G$ such that

$$\min_\tau\{v_{\sigma,\tau}(start(G_{\sigma,\tau}))\} > \frac{1}{2} \ ,$$

where $G_{\sigma,\tau}$ is the subgraph of $G$ with respect to policies $\sigma$ and $\tau$.

We now describe the nondeterministic Turing machine $M'$ which accepts the same language as $M$. On input $x$, $M'$ constructs the graph $G$ which represents $M$ on input $x$. Then $M'$ existentially chooses an existential policy $\sigma$ of $G$, and computes

$$\min_\tau\{v_{\sigma,\tau}(start(G_{\sigma,\tau}))\} \ .$$

If this quantity is $> \frac{1}{2}$ then $M'$ accepts $x$; otherwise $M'$ rejects $x$.

Clearly $M'$ accepts $x$ if and only if $M$ accepts $x$. It remains to show that $M'$ runs in time $2^{O(s(n))}$. We show that on an input of length $n$, $M'$ runs in time polynomial in $N$, the number of nodes in the graph representing $M$ on $x$. Since $N = 2^{O(s(n))}$, this implies that $M$ runs in time $2^{O(s(n))}$.

Since $G$ has $N$ nodes, $M$ requires time at most polynomial in $N$ to construct $G$ and to choose a policy $\sigma$ of $G$. We need to show that $\min_{\tau}\{v_{\sigma,\tau}(start(G_\sigma))\}$ can be computed in time polynomial in $N$. We claim that this is the value $v(start(G_{\sigma,\tau}))$ where for $1 \leq i \leq N$, $v(i)$ is the optimal solution to the following linear programming problem: maximize $\sum_{i=1}^{N} v(i)$, subject to the constraints

$v(i) = 0$, if $i = N - 1$,
$v(i) = 1$, if $i = N$,
$v(i) \geq \frac{1}{2}(v(j) + v(k))$,
  if $i$ is a coin-tossing node of $G_\sigma$ with outgoing edges $(i, j), (i, k)$,
$v(i) \leq v(j)$,
  if $i$ is an existential or universal node of $G_\sigma$ with outgoing edge $(i, j)$.

The proof of this claim is similar to the proof of Lemma 4.13. Since the linear programming problem can be solved in time polynomial in $N$, just as in Theorem 4.13, $M'$ uses time polynomial in $N$. Hence $\forall UC\text{--}SPACE(s(n)) \subseteq \bigcup_{c \geq 0} NTIME(2^{cs(n)})$. $\square$

To complete this section, we summarize the best known results on logarithmic space bounded game automata of complete information with both randomness and universal moves.

**Theorem 4.17**

$$P \subseteq \forall BC\text{--}SPACE(\log n) \subseteq \forall UC\text{--}SPACE(\log n) \subseteq NP .$$

**Proof:** The fact that $P \subseteq \forall BC\text{--}SPACE(\log n)$ follows from Theorem 4.6, since $P = ASPACE(\log n)$ [9]. $\forall BC\text{--}SPACE(\log n) \subseteq \forall UC\text{--}SPACE(\log n)$ since a bounded random game automaton is trivially an unbounded random game automaton. Finally, Theorem 4.16 shows that $\forall UC\text{--}SPACE(\log n) \subseteq NP$. $\square$

# 5

## Space Bounded Game Automata with Partial Information

We present in this chapter some results on space bounded game automata with partial information. In Section 5.1 we compare space bounded game automata with complete information to those with partial information. We show that partial information increases the complexity of space bounded game automata since for space constructible $s(n) = \Omega(n)$,

$$BC\text{--}SPACE(s(n)) \subseteq BP\text{--}SPACE(\log(s(n))) . \qquad (5.1)$$

This result shows that the languages accepted by polynomial space bounded Arthur-Merlin games is contained in the class of log space bounded interactive proof systems. Combining this result with the results of Chapter 4, it follows that any language in deterministic exponential time can be proved interactively in log space. The result also implies that the class of languages accepted by polynomial space bounded games against nature is contained in the class of languages accepted by logarithmic space bounded games against unknown nature.

Unlike the game automata we have considered in previous chapters, we do not have a complete characterization of the class of languages accepted by space bounded game automata with partial information. We cannot show, for example, that Equation 5.1 can be strengthened to $BP\text{--}SPACE(\log(s(n))) = BC\text{--}SPACE(s(n))$. One reason that game automata with partial information are hard to characterize is that on some inputs accepted by such a game automaton, player 1 of $M$ may not have a winning strategy that is Markov. We will see an example in a later proof of an $s(n)$ space bounded game automaton $M$ in the class $BP$ and input $x$, such that $M$ accepts $x$ by the definitions given in Chapter 2 but such that player 1 has no Markov strategy that has value $> \frac{1}{2}$ on input $x$.

However this reason alone is not what makes space bounded game automata hard to characterize. In fact Reif and Peterson [30], [28] completely characterized space bounded game automata with partial information with no randomness, that is, space bounded game automata in the class $\forall P$. They showed that $\forall P\text{--}SPACE(\log s(n)) = \forall C\text{--}SPACE(s(n))$. It is the combination of randomness with non-Markov strategies that is hard to analyze. We discuss this in more detail in Section 5.2. We also present there some results that characterize space bounded game automata where the strategy of player 1 is restricted to depend only on a limited history. The amount of history on which player 1's strategy depends is counted as a resource, just as space or time. In Chapter 2 we defined a game automaton that is $h(n)$ history bounded as follows. A strategy $\sigma$ on input $x$ has *history* bound $h$ if $\sigma(visible(H_1, 1)) = \sigma(visible(H_2, 1))$ for any pair of histories of $M$ on $x$ such that the sequence consisting of the last $h$ visible configurations of $visible(H_1, 1)$ and the corresponding sequence of $visible(H_2, 1))$ are the same. A game automaton $M$ with bound $\epsilon$ is $h(n)$ history bounded if for every $n$ and every input of length $n$ accepted by $M$, there is a strategy $\sigma$ of $M$ that has history bound $h(n)$ and such that $v_\sigma > \frac{1}{2} + \epsilon$. If $M$ has history bound 1 then we say $M$ is a *Markov game automaton*.

We consider game automata with simultaneous space and history bounds. We denote the class of languages accepted by unbounded random game automata that have simultaneous space bound $s(n)$ and history bound $h(n)$ by $UP\text{--}SPACE, HIS(s(n), h(n))$. For the special case of Markov game automata, we denote the class $G\text{--}SPACE, HIS(s(n), 1)$, where $G$ is any type of game automaton, by $GM\text{--}SPACE(s(n))$. We show that space bounded Markov game automata automata recognize the same languages as nondeterministic Turing machines that run in time exponential in $s(n)$. Thus for space constructible $s(n) = \Omega(\log n)$,

$$\cup_c NTIME(2^{cs(n)}) \;=\; BM\text{--}SPACE(s(n)) = UM\text{--}SPACE(s(n))$$
$$=\; \forall BM\text{--}SPACE(s(n)) = \forall UM\text{--}SPACE(s(n)) \;.$$

Secondly we show that the history bound of a game automaton can be decreased at the cost of increasing the space. If $h(n)$ is a space constructible function then

$$UP\text{--}SPACE, HIS(s(n), h(n)) \subseteq UP\text{--}SPACE, HIS(s(n) + h(n), O(1)) \ .$$

This result and other results on game automata with simultaneous space and history bounds, including Markov game automata, are presented in Section 5.2.

# 5.1   Using Partial Information to Reduce Space

The purpose of this section is to show that space bounded game automata with partial information are more powerful than space bounded game automata with complete information. We start by showing that the class of languages accepted by $\log s(n)$ space bounded games against unknown nature contains any language accepted by an $s(n)$ space bounded game against nature. After this proof we show how variations of the same proof show similar results for other space bounded probabilistic game automata classes.

**Theorem 5.1** *If* $s(n) = \Omega(n)$ *is constructible,*

$$UC\text{--}SPACE(s(n)) \subseteq UP\text{--}SPACE(\log s(n)) \ .$$

**Proof:** Reif [30] proved a similar result for game automata without randomness; he showed that $\forall C\text{--}SPACE(s(n)) \subseteq \forall P\text{--}SPACE(\log s(n))$. The simulation in the proof we present is similar to Reif's, though the proof is more complicated here. Let $M$ be an $s(n)$ space bounded game automaton in the class $UC$. In order to prove our result, we assume that $M$ is a one-tape automaton and that the players alternate moves, starting with player 0. We describe a $\log s(n)$ space bounded game automaton $M'$ in the class $UP$ that simulates $M$.

Intuitively the simulation works as follows. Fix some input $x$ of length $n$. Player $1'$ of $M'$ existentially simulates a history of $M$ on $x$ by listing each symbol of the history in sequence. If player $1'$ lists a halting configuration at some step, $M'$ halts in an accepting state if and only if the configuration is accepting. Player $0'$ checks that the sequence of symbols listed by player $1'$ is a valid history of $M$ and halts in a rejecting state if the history is not valid. Since player $0'$ is bounded by $O(\log n)$ space, it cannot check the complete history listed by player $1'$. The key idea is that player $0'$ *randomly and privately* decides whether to check one symbol of the history. After each step where player $1'$ has listed a symbol of the history, player $0'$ checks the symbol with probability $\frac{3}{4}$. Once player $0'$ has checked a symbol, the computation halts. With probability $\frac{1}{4}$ player $0'$ does not check the symbol and player $1'$ lists the next symbol of the history. Since player $1'$ does not know when player $0'$ is checking the listing, it is forced to output a valid history.

We now describe in more detail how player $1'$ lists a history of $M$. A history can be represented as a string $m_0 a_1 m_1 \ldots a_i m_i \ldots$, where each $m_i$ is a configuration and $m_0$ is the initial configuration. Each $a_i \in \{1, 2\}$ and $m_{i-1} \overset{a_i}{\to} m_i$ for $i > 0$, that is, the $a_i th$ possible next configuration from $m_{i-1}$ is $m_i$, according to the transition function of $M$. Each configuration $m_i$ is represented as a string $c_1 \ldots c_{k-1} \, q \, c_k \ldots c_{s(n)}$, where $q$ is a state of $M$, $c_1 \ldots c_{s(n)}$ represents the contents of the worktape and the tape head is positioned on the $k th$ tape cell. Each $c_i$ is either an input symbol, a worktape symbol or a special blank symbol. The length of each $m_i$ is $s(n) + 1$. The initial configuration $m_0$ is represented as the string $q_0 x \, \slashed{b}^{s(n)-|x|}$ where $q_0$ is the initial state. In this case the string $c_1 \ldots c_n$ represents the input, for $n < i \le s(n)$ $c_i$ is the blank symbol $\slashed{b}$ and $k = 1$.

Let the visible substates of $M'$ contain the worktape and input alphabet of $M$, the blank symbol and the set $\{1, 2\}$. In one step, player $1'$ lists a symbol in the string $m_0 a_1 m_1 \ldots$ by entering the visible substate that corresponds to the symbol. Thus, player $1'$ does not use any space at all. In order to list the symbol $a_i \in \{1, 2\}$ when $m_{i-1}$ is a coin-tossing configuration, player $1'$ changes the value of the turn indicator and player $0'$ takes a coin-tossing step. Thus $a_i$ is chosen randomly and uniformly if $i$ is odd and is chosen existentially if $i$ is even. As a result, player $1'$ lists $a_i$ as a 1 or 2 with equal probability.

Next we show how player $0'$ checks that the string listed by player $1'$ is a valid history of $M$. The string listed by player $1'$ is *valid* if it satisfies the following conditions:

- $m_0$ is the initial configuration of $M$ and each $m_i$ has length $s(n) + 1$,

- if $m_{i-1}$ is a coin-tossing configuration then $a_i$ is chosen randomly by player $0'$ and if $m_{i-1}$ is an existential configuration then $a_i$ is chosen by player $1'$, where $a_i \in \{1, 2\}$ and

- $m_{i-1} \xrightarrow{a_i} m_i$ for $i > 0$, that is, $m_i$ is the $a_i th$ possible configuration reachable from $m_{i-1}$ according to the transition function.

To check the first condition, player $0'$ verifies that $m_0 = q_0 x \not b^{s(n)-|x|}$. Player $0'$ can verify in $\log s(n)$ space that each $m_i$ has length $s(n) + 1$, since $s(n)$ is space constructible and $s(n) = \Omega(n)$. To check that $a_i$ is chosen correctly for some $i$, player $0'$ needs to verify that $a_i \in \{1, 2\}$ and that $a_i$ is determined as a result of a coin-tossing step of player $0'$ if the turn indicator of configuration $m_{i-1}$ is 0. If player $0'$ ever finds that either of the first two conditions is not satisfied, it halts in a rejecting state. To check the last condition, player $0'$ would need to write down on a tape configuration $m_{i-1}$ while configuration $m_i$ is being listed by player $1'$, in order to check that there is a valid transition from $m_{i-1}$ to $m_i$. Thus player $0'$ cannot check the last condition since each $m_i$ is of length $s(n) + 1$ and player $0'$ can use space only $O(\log s(n))$. However, player $0'$ can check *one* symbol of a configuration as follows. Suppose that player $0'$ decides to check the $kth$ symbol of $m_i$, $i > 0$. Then player $0'$ stores on a private tape the four symbols numbered $k - 1, k, k + 1, k + 2$ of configuration $m_{i-1}$, together with $k$ and $a_i$. Using this information and the transition function of $M$, player $0'$ can verify that the $kth$ symbol of $m_i$ is valid. Player $0'$ uses $O(\log s(n))$ space to store $k$ and constant space to store $a_i$ and the four symbols. The definition of a *valid symbol* follows naturally from the definition of a valid string given by the three conditions above. Player $0'$ can check if any symbol of the string listed by player $1'$ is valid, using only $O(\log s(n))$ space.

Player $0'$ privately and randomly decides to check one symbol of the history listed by player $1'$ (excluding the initial configuration and the $a_i$) in the following way. Suppose player $1'$ lists a symbol, say symbol $k-1$ of configuration $m_{i-1}$ and player $0'$ has not already chosen a symbol to check. Then with probability $\frac{3}{4}$ player $0'$ decides to check symbol $k$ of configuration $m_i$ and decides not to check with probability $\frac{1}{4}$. If player $0'$ decides to check, it records $k$, the symbol just listed by player $1'$ and the next three symbols player $1'$ lists. When player $1'$ lists $a_i$ player $0'$ also records its value. Then at a later time when player $1'$ lists the $kth$ symbol of $m_i$, player $0'$ actually checks that the symbol is valid. If the symbol is valid, player $0'$ halts, accepting with probability $\frac{1}{2}$

and rejecting with probability $\frac{1}{2}$. Otherwise the symbol is invalid and player $0'$ halts in a rejecting state. If player $0'$ does not decide to check the symbol, player $1'$ lists the next symbol and player $0'$ repeats the same process. It is crucial to the proof that player $1'$ does not know whether player $0'$ has decided to check a symbol or not.

We summarize this description of $M'$ in the algorithms of Figures 5.2 and 5.1. In the algorithms, the Boolean variable *checking* is true if and only if player $0'$ has decided to check a symbol of some configuration $m_i$ for $i > 1$. The variable $k$ records which symbol of the current configuration is being listed by player $1'$. The variable *initial* is true only when the first configuration is being listed by player $1'$. It is used by player $0'$ so that it can check that the initial configuration is correctly listed by player $1'$. The variable *oddconfiguration* is true when the configuration listed by player $1'$ is an odd numbered configuration. This is used by player $0'$ so it can randomly choose $a_i$ for configurations where it is player 0's turn. The variable *checkcount* is used to keep track of which symbols listed by player $1'$ need to be recorded by player $0'$, and also when the symbol to be checked is actually listed. The variable *symbol* denotes the symbol most recently listed by player $1'$.

**procedure** *generalcheck*;
    if **not** *checking* <u>then</u>
        with probability $\frac{3}{4}$ *checking* := true; *checkcount* := 0;

    if *checking* <u>then</u>
        *checkcount* := *checkcount* +1;
        <u>if</u> *checkcount* $\in \{1, \ldots, 4\}$    <u>then</u> record *symbol*;
        <u>if</u> $k = s(n) + 1$           <u>then</u> record *symbol* $a_i$;
        <u>if</u> *checkcount* $= s(n) + 1$    <u>then</u> check *symbol* is valid;
            <u>if</u> not valid <u>then</u> reject
                      <u>else</u> halt, accepting with probability $\frac{1}{2}$

Figure 5.1: *General checking procedure, Theorem 5.1.*

**procedure** main-algorithm;
<u>begin</u>
/* initialization */
*oddconfiguration* := false; *checking* := false;
$k := 0$; *initial* := true;
<u>repeat</u>
    Player 0': visibly do the following:
        $k := k + 1 \pmod{s(n) + 2}$;
        <u>if</u> $k = s(n) + 1$ <u>then</u>
            *oddconfiguration* := **not**(*oddconfiguration*);
            <u>if</u> *oddconfiguration* <u>then</u> with probability $\frac{1}{2}$ $a_i := 1$, <u>else</u> $a_i := 2$;

    Player 1': existentially list the next *symbol* of the history being simulated;

    Player 0': Privately do the following:

        /* check initial configuration */
        <u>if</u> *initial* <u>then</u>
            <u>if</u> $k = 1$ <u>then</u>
                if *symbol* is not the initial state, reject;
            <u>if</u> $1 < k \le n + 1$ <u>then</u>
                if *symbol* is not the $(k-1)$st input bit, reject;
            <u>if</u> $n + 1 < k \le s(n) + 1$ <u>then</u>
                if *symbol* is not the blank symbol, reject;
            <u>if</u> $k = s(n) + 1$ <u>then</u>
                *initial* := false;

        <u>if</u> $(k = s(n) + 1)$ **and** (*oddconfiguration*) <u>then</u>
            check that *symbol* equals $a_i$; if not, reject;

        <u>if</u> $(k = s(n) + 1)$ **and** (**not** *oddconfiguration*) <u>then</u>
            check that *symbol* $\in \{1, 2\}$; if not, reject;

        /* execute general checking procedure */
        *generalcheck*;
<u>until</u> the last symbol of the history is listed;
<u>if</u> the state of the last configuration listed is accepting <u>then</u>
    halt and accept
<u>else</u> reject
<u>end</u>

Figure 5.2: *Main algorithm of Theorem 5.1.*

Before getting to the proof that $M'$ accepts the same language as $M$ and that $M'$ is an unbounded random game automaton, we introduce some notation. Fix an arbitrary input $x$. Let $\sigma'$ be any strategy of player $1'$ on $x$. If the string listed by player $1'$ on strategy $\sigma'$ on *any* sequence of coin tosses of player $0'$ is valid, we say $\sigma'$ is a *valid* strategy. Otherwise $\sigma'$ is an *invalid* strategy. Each valid strategy $\sigma'$ of player $1'$ corresponds to a strategy of player $1$ in a natural way which we now describe. Let $H$ be a history of $M$ ending in an existential configuration and let $m_0 a_1 m_1 \ldots a_i m_i$ represent history $H$, where $i$ is odd. Then if player $1'$ on strategy $\sigma'$ lists $a_{i+1} m_{i+1}$ after listing $m_0 a_1 \ldots a_i m_i$, define $\sigma(H) = C_{i+1}$ where $C_{i+1}$ is the configuration represented by $m_{i+1}$. We say $\sigma'$ *simulates* the strategy $\sigma$ derived in this way from $\sigma'$.

Just as we distinguish between two types of steps of player $1'$, we also distinguish between two types of steps of player $0'$. At each turn, if player $0'$ has not already decided to check a symbol during the current simulation, player $0'$ takes either of two actions. With probability $\frac{3}{4}$ it checks that a symbol to be listed later by player $1'$ is valid. Alternatively, with probability $\frac{1}{4}$ it decides not to check. We call a history of $M'$ where player $0'$ checks a symbol a *checking history*. A history of $M'$ where player $0'$ does not check a symbol is called a *non-checking history*. Each path of a computation tree $T_{\sigma'}$ is labeled by a history. If the history is a checking history, then the corresponding path in the computation tree is called a checking path; otherwise the path is called a non-checking path. If $\sigma'$ simulates $\sigma$ then each non-checking path of $T_{\sigma'}$ is a simulation of some history of $M$; there is a one-to-one correspondence between the non-checking paths of $T_{\sigma'}$ and the paths of $T_{\sigma}$.

We need to show that player $1'$ has a unbounded winning strategy on input $x$ if and only if player $1$ does, and that if all strategies of player $1$ are unbounded losing strategies, then so also are all strategies of player $1'$. The bulk of the proof is divided into the following two claims.

**Claim 5.2** *Let $M$ and $M'$ be defined as above and let $\sigma'$ be a strategy of $M'$ on $x$ that simulates strategy $\sigma$ of $M$. Then $v_{\sigma'} > \frac{1}{2}$ if and only if $v_\sigma > \frac{1}{2}$. That is, the probability that $M'$ halts in an accepting state on $x$ when player $1'$ uses strategy $\sigma'$ is $> \frac{1}{2}$ if and only if the probability that $M$ accepts $x$ when player $1$ uses strategy $\sigma$ is $> \frac{1}{2}$.*

**Claim 5.3** *Let $M$ and $M'$ be defined as above and let $\sigma'$ be an invalid strategy of $M'$ on $x$. Then there is a valid strategy $\psi$ of $M'$ such that $v_{\sigma'} \leq v_\psi$.*

Before proving these claims, we show how they can be combined to prove the theorem. Suppose $M$ accepts $x$. Then some strategy $\sigma$ of $M$ on $x$ is an unbounded winning strategy, hence $v_\sigma > \frac{1}{2}$. From Claim 5.2, $v_{\sigma'} > \frac{1}{2}$ where $\sigma'$ is the strategy of $M'$ that simulates $\sigma$. Hence $\sigma'$ is an unbounded winning strategy and so $M'$ accepts $x$. The other case to consider is when $M$ rejects $x$. Then for all strategies $\sigma$ of $M$, $v_\sigma \leq \frac{1}{2}$. From Claim 5.2 it follows that all valid strategies $\sigma'$ of player $1'$ must be unbounded losing strategies. Furthermore by Claim 5.3, all invalid strategies of $M'$ must also be unbounded losing strategies and so $x$ is rejected by $M'$. Hence $M'$ is an unbounded random automaton and $M'$ accepts the same language as $M$. We now turn to the proofs of the claims.

**Proof of Claim 5.2:** Assume that $\sigma'$ of $M'$ is a valid strategy and that it simulates strategy $\sigma$ of $M$. Note that $v_{\sigma'}$ is the value of the computation tree $T_{\sigma'}$. Recall that we partitioned the paths of $T_{\sigma'}$ into two types: checking paths and non-checking paths. The probability of reaching an accepting state given that a checking path of $T_{\sigma'}$ is followed is $\frac{1}{2}$. This is because player $0'$ halts in an accepting state with probability $\frac{1}{2}$ whenever it checks a symbol. The probability of reaching an accepting state given that a non-checking path of $T_{\sigma'}$ is followed is $v_\sigma$. This is because of the one-to-one correspondence between the non-checking paths of $T_{\sigma'}$ and the paths of $T_\sigma$.

Let $p_{check}$ be the probability that player $0'$ checks a symbol listed by player $1'$, that is, $p_{check}$ is the probability of following a checking path of $T_{\sigma'}$. Then $v_{\sigma'}$ is

$$v_{\sigma'} = p_{check}\frac{1}{2} + (1 - p_{check})v_\sigma = \frac{1}{2} + (1 - p_{check})(v_\sigma - \frac{1}{2}) \ .$$

This is greater than $\frac{1}{2}$ if and only if $v_\sigma > \frac{1}{2}$, as required. This completes the proof of Claim 5.2. $\square$

**Proof of Claim 5.3:** This claim states that given an invalid strategy $\sigma'$, there is some valid strategy that is at least as good. Intuitively this is true because there is a stiff penalty for player $1'$ when it lists an invalid symbol; if player $0'$ checks that symbol, the game automaton halts in a rejecting state. This intuition suggests that by redefining $\sigma'$ so that player $1'$ always lists valid symbols instead of invalid symbols, we get a strategy that has value at least as great as the value of $\sigma'$.

We first show how to construct a strategy $\psi$, that is valid and is the same as $\sigma'$ on valid histories. Later we argue that the strategy $\psi$ has value at least as great as $v_{\sigma'}$. Without loss of generality we only consider invalid strategies of player $1'$ that satisfy the first two conditions of a valid strategy. That is, if $m_0$ is the initial configuration of $M$, each $m_i$ has length $s(n) + 1$. Also if $m_{i-1}$ is a coin-tossing configuration then $a_i$ is chosen randomly by player $0'$ and if $m_{i-1}$ is an existential configuration then $a_i$ is chosen by player $1'$, where $a_i \in \{1, 2\}$. On any history of the game automaton where player $1'$ does not satisfy the first two conditions the game automaton always halts in a rejecting state, since player $0'$ always checks that these conditions are satisfied. Thus let $\sigma'$ be a strategy of player $1'$ which does not satisfy the third condition, which is that for all $i$, $m_i$ is the $a_i$th possible configuration reachable from $m_{i-1}$ according to the transition function.

Let $\phi$ be any valid strategy of $M'$. Let $\mathcal{VH}$ be the set of valid visible histories $VH$ such that in the transition from $VH$ to $\sigma'(VH)$, player $1'$ lists an invalid symbol. We obtain a new strategy $\psi$ by defining $\psi$ to be the same as $\phi$ on visible histories that have a prefix in $\mathcal{VH}$. We let $\psi$ be the same as $\sigma'$ on all other histories. Formally,

$$\psi(visible(H, 1')) = \begin{cases} \phi(visible(H, 1')), \\ \quad \text{if some } VH \in \mathcal{VH} \text{ is a prefix of } visible(H, 1'), \\ \sigma'(visible(H, 1')), \text{otherwise} . \end{cases}$$

It is easy to see that $\psi$ is well-defined and is valid. It remains to prove that $v_\psi \geq v_{\sigma'}$. We first derive an expression for $v_\psi - v_{\sigma'}$ in terms of the visible histories in $\mathcal{VH}$. For $VH \in \mathcal{VH}$, let $prob[VH]$ be the probability of following a path of $T_{\sigma'}$ which is labeled by a history with visible prefix $VH$. Then $prob[VH]$ is also the probability of following a path of $T_\psi$ which is labeled by a history with visible prefix $VH$. This is because the computation trees $T_\psi$ and $T_{\sigma'}$ are identical on paths which are labeled by valid visible histories, and each $VH$ is a valid visible history. Let $accept[\sigma', VH]$ denote the conditional probability of reaching an accepting leaf of $T_{\sigma'}$, given that a path is followed that is labeled by a history with visible prefix $VH$. Similarly define $accept[\psi, VH]$. We claim that

$$v_\psi - v_{\sigma'} = \sum_{VH \in \mathcal{VH}} prob[VH]( accept[\psi, VH] - accept[\sigma', VH] ) .$$

To see this, first note that the strategies $\psi$ and $\sigma'$ differ only on visible histories which have prefix $VH$ for some $VH \in \mathcal{VH}$. From the definitions of

$accept[\sigma', VH]$ and $accept[\psi, VH]$, it follows that $accept[\psi, VH] - accept[\sigma', VH]$ is the difference in the probability that an accepting leaf is reached in computation tree $T_\psi$ and the probability that an accepting state is reached in computation tree $T_{\sigma'}$, when following a path of each tree which is labeled by a history with visible prefix $VH$. Thirdly, the probabilities $prob[VH]$ and $prob[VH']$ are independent for distinct $VH, VH' \in \mathcal{VH}$. Hence by adding the terms $prob[VH]( accept[\psi, VH] - accept[\sigma', VH] )$ for all $VH \in \mathcal{VH}$, the total difference between $v_\psi$ and $v_{\sigma'}$ is obtained.

We now show that $accept[\psi, VH] - accept[\sigma', VH] > 0$ for any visible history $VH \in \mathcal{VH}$. Fix some $VH \in \mathcal{VH}$. Suppose the symbol listed by player $1'$ in the transition from $VH$ to $\sigma'(VH)$ is the $kth$ symbol of $m_i$ for some $k$ and $i$. If $VH$ has occurred, player $0'$ cannot have decided to check any symbol listed *before* the $kth$ symbol of $m_i$. This is because as soon as player $0'$ checks a symbol, it halts, and player $1'$ lists no further symbols. Since player $0'$ has not already decided to check a symbol, the probability that player $0'$ checks the $kth$ symbol of $m_i$ is $\frac{3}{4}$. If player $0'$ checks this symbol, it halts in a rejecting state when player $1'$ uses strategy $\sigma'$ because player $1'$ lists an invalid symbol in the transition from $VH$ to $\sigma'(VH)$. This proves that $accept[\sigma', VH] \leq \frac{1}{4}$.

In a similar way, we prove that $\frac{1}{4} < accept[\psi, VH]$. If player $1'$ uses strategy $\psi$, it lists a valid symbol in the transition from $VH$ to $\psi(VH)$. With probability $\frac{3}{4}$ player $0'$ checks that the symbol is valid and if it is, it halts in an accepting state with probability $\frac{1}{2}$. This means that the probability $M$ halts in an accepting state is $\geq \frac{3}{4}\frac{1}{2} > \frac{1}{4}$ and so $\frac{1}{4} < accept[\psi, VH]$. We have now shown that for any $VH \in \mathcal{VH}$, $accept[\sigma', VH] \leq \frac{1}{4} < accept[\psi, VH]$. Since $prob[VH] \geq 0$ for all $VH \in \mathcal{VH}$, it follows that

$$v_\psi - v_{\sigma'} = \sum_{VH \in \mathcal{VH}} prob[VH]( accept[\psi, VH] - accept[\sigma', VH] ) \geq 0 .$$

This completes the proof that $v_\psi \geq v_{\sigma'}$, and so the claim is proved. $\square$

**Theorem 5.4** *For space constructible,* $s(n) = \Omega(n)$,

$$BC\text{--}SPACE(s(n)) \subseteq BP\text{--}SPACE(\log s(n)) .$$

**Proof:** The proof of this is very similar to the proof of Theorem 5.1. Let $M$ be a game automaton in the class $BC$ that is $s(n)$ space bounded. We make two assumptions about $M$. First, we assume that $M$ is a one-tape automaton. Second, we assume that $M$ accepts every input with probability $\geq \frac{1}{4}$ and that the bound of $M$ is $\frac{7}{16}$. We show that this assumption can be made without loss of generality. Given an arbitrary bounded random game automaton $M'$ with bound $\frac{1}{4}$, we can easily construct a bounded random game automaton $M$ that accepts the same language as $M'$ and has the above properties. On any input, player 0 of $M$ initially tosses two coins. If the outcome of both coin tosses is heads, player 0 halts in an accepting state. Otherwise the players of $M$ simulate the players of $M'$.

We describe a game automaton $M'$ that recognizes the same language as $M$. Intuitively the simulation of $M'$ by $M$ works as follows. Fix some input $x$ of length $n$. Player $1'$ of $M'$ existentially simulates a history of $M$ on $x$ by listing each symbol of the history in sequence. If player $1'$ lists a halting configuration at some step, $M'$ halts in an accepting state if and only if the configuration is accepting. Player $0'$ checks that the sequence of symbols listed by player $1'$ is a valid history of $M$ and halts in a rejecting state if the history is not valid. To do this, player $0'$ randomly and privately decides whether to check one symbol of the history. After each step where player $1'$ has listed a symbol of the history, player $0'$ checks the symbol with probability $\frac{7}{8}$. The difference between this simulation and the simulation of Theorem 5.1 is that if player $0'$ checks a symbol of the history that is valid, then the simulation starts from scratch again. Just as in the simulation of Theorem 5.1, if the symbol is invalid, player $0'$ halts in a rejecting state. With probability $\frac{1}{8}$ player $0'$ does not check the symbol and player $1'$ lists the next symbol of the history. Since player $1'$ does not know when player $0'$ is checking the listing, it is forced to output a valid history.

The way player $1'$ lists a history of $M$ is the same as in Theorem 5.1. Briefly, a history is represented as a string $m_0 a_1 m_1 \ldots a_i m_i \ldots$, where each $m_i$ is a configuration, $m_0$ is the initial configuration, each $a_i \in \{1, 2\}$ and $m_{i-1} \xrightarrow{a_i} m_i$ for $i > 0$. Each configuration $m_i$ is represented as a string $c_1 \ldots c_{k-1} \, q \, c_k \ldots c_{s(n)}$, where $q$ is a state of $M$, $c_1 \ldots c_{s(n)}$ represents the contents of the worktape and the tape head is positioned on the $k$th tape cell.

The way that player $0'$ checks that the history listed by player $1'$ is valid is also very similar to the description in Theorem 5.1. Player $0'$ checks the symbols of the initial configuration and the $a_i$ of the history listed by player $1'$ just as in Theorem 5.1. Player $0'$ privately and randomly decides to check the other symbols of the history in the following way. Suppose player $1'$ lists a symbol, say symbol $k-1$ of configuration $m_{i-1}$ and player $0'$ has not already chosen a symbol to check. Then with probability $\frac{7}{8}$ player $0'$ decides to check symbol $k$ of configuration $m_i$ and with probability $\frac{1}{8}$ it decides not to check this symbol. In the case that player $0'$ decides to check, it records $k$, the symbol just listed by player $1'$ and the next three symbols player $1'$ lists. When player $1'$ lists $a_i$ player $0'$ also records its value. Then at a later time when player $1'$ lists the $kth$ symbol of $m_i$, player $0'$ actually checks that the symbol is valid. If the symbol is valid, player $0'$ starts the simulation from scratch. Otherwise the symbol is invalid and player $0'$ halts in a rejecting state. If player $0'$ does not decide to check the symbol (which happens with probability $\frac{1}{8}$), player $1'$ lists the next symbol and player $0'$ repeats the same process to decide whether to start checking.

The only difference between this simulation and the simulation of Theorem 5.1 is in the general checking procedure of player $0'$, which we present in Figure 5.3. The remainder of the algorithm is exactly as in Figure 5.2.

It is straightforward to check that $M'$ uses space $O(\log s(n))$. It remains to show that $M$ and $M'$ accept the same language. We need to show that player $1'$ has a bounded winning strategy on input $x$ if and only if player 1 does, and that if all strategies of player 1 are bounded losing strategies, then so also are all strategies of player $1'$. Fix an arbitrary input $x$. We define a valid, invalid and a simulating strategy of player $1'$ just as in Theorem 5.1. The proof is divided into the following three claims.

**Claim 5.5** *Let $M$ and $M'$ be defined as above. If $\sigma'$ is a strategy of $M'$ on $x$ that simulates strategy $\sigma$ of $M$, then $v_\sigma = v_{\sigma'}$. That is, the probability that $M'$ halts in an accepting state on $x$ when player $1'$ uses strategy $\sigma'$ equals the probability that $M$ accepts $x$ when player 1 uses strategy $\sigma$.*

**Claim 5.6** *If $x$ is not accepted by $M$ then every valid strategy of $M'$ on $x$ is a bounded losing strategy.*

**Claim 5.7** *Let $M$, $M'$ be defined as above and let $\sigma'$ be an invalid strategy of $M'$ on $x$. Then there is a valid strategy $\psi$ of $M'$ such that $v_{\sigma'} \leq v_\psi$.*

**procedure** *generalcheck*;
    <u>if</u> **not** *checking* <u>then</u>
        with probability $\frac{7}{8}$ *checking* := true; *checkcount* := 0;

    <u>if</u> *checking* <u>then</u>
        *checkcount* := *checkcount* +1;
        <u>if</u> *checkcount* $\in \{1, \ldots, 4\}$   <u>then</u> record *symbol*;
        <u>if</u> $k = s(n) + 1$          <u>then</u> record *symbol* $a_i$;
        <u>if</u> *checkcount* $= s(n) + 1$   <u>then</u> check *symbol* is valid;
            <u>if</u> **not** valid <u>then</u> reject
            <u>else</u>
                /* restart simulation; */
                /* set all variables to initial values */
                *oddconfiguration* := false;
                *checking* := false;
                $k$ := 0;
                *initial* := true;
                move all tape heads to inital position

Figure 5.3: *General checking procedure, Theorem 5.4.*

Before proving these claims, we show how they can be combined to prove the theorem. Suppose $M$ accepts $x$. Then some strategy $\sigma$ of $M$ on $x$ is a bounded winning strategy. The error probability of $M$ is $\frac{7}{16}$, hence $v_\sigma > \frac{9}{16}$. From Claim 5.5, $v_{\sigma'} > \frac{9}{16}$ where $\sigma'$ is the strategy of $M'$ that simulates $\sigma$. Hence $\sigma'$ is a bounded winning strategy and so $M'$ accepts $x$. The other case to consider is when $M$ rejects $x$. Then for all strategies $\sigma$ of $M$, $v_\sigma < \frac{7}{16}$. From Claim 5.5 it follows that all valid strategies $\sigma'$ of player $1'$ must be bounded losing strategies. Furthermore by Claim 5.7, all invalid strategies of $M'$ must also be bounded losing strategies and so $x$ is rejected by $M$. Hence $M'$ is a bounded random game automaton and $M'$ accepts the same language as $M$. We now turn to the proofs of the claims.

**Proof of Claim 5.5:** Assume that $\sigma'$ of $M'$ is a valid strategy and that it simulates strategy $\sigma$ of $M$ on $x$. Note that $v_{\sigma'}$ is the value of the computation tree $T_{\sigma'}$. Recall that we partitioned the paths of $T_{\sigma'}$ into two types: checking paths and non-checking paths. The probability of reaching an accepting state given that a checking path of $T_{\sigma'}$ is followed is $v_{\sigma'}$. This is because the simulation is started again when player $0'$ checks a symbol. The probability of reaching an accepting state given that a non-checking path of $T_{\sigma'}$ is followed is $v_\sigma$. This is because of the one-to-one correspondence between the non-checking paths of $T_{\sigma'}$ and the paths of $T_\sigma$.

Let $p_{check}$ be the probability that player $0'$ checks a symbol listed by player $1'$, that is, $p_{check}$ is the probability of following a checking path of $T_{\sigma'}$. Then $v_{\sigma'}$ is

$$v_{\sigma'} = p_{check} v_{\sigma'} + (1 - p_{check}) v_\sigma$$

$$\Rightarrow v_{\sigma'} = v_\sigma .$$

This completes the proof of Claim 5.5. $\square$

**Proof of Claim 5.6:** Let $\sigma_{opt}$ be an optimal strategy of $M$. By an optimal strategy we mean one which has value greater than or equal to any other strategy of player 1. In a space bounded game of complete information an optimal strategy exists since there are only finitely many Markov strategies and one of those must be optimal. It is straightforward to show that the value of any valid strategy is at most the value of the strategy of player $1'$ that simulates an optimal strategy of player 1. Let this strategy of player $1'$ be $\sigma'_{opt}$. From Claim 5.5, $v_{\sigma'_{opt}} = v_{\sigma_{opt}}$. Since $x$ is not accepted by $M'$, $\sigma_{opt}$ must be a bounded losing strategy. Hence $v_{\sigma_{opt}} < \frac{7}{16}$ and so $v_{\sigma'_{opt}} < \frac{7}{16}$. Thus $\sigma'_{opt}$ is a bounded losing strategy of $M'$, and hence so is any valid strategy of $M'$. $\square$.

**Proof of Claim 5.7:** Again, the proof of this is very similar to the proof of Claim 5.3. We first show how to construct a strategy $\psi$, which is valid and is the same as $\sigma'$ on valid histories. Later we argue that the strategy $v_\psi \geq v_{\sigma'}$. Without loss of generality we only consider invalid strategies of player $1'$ which satisfy the first two conditions of a valid strategy. On any history of the game automaton where player $1'$ does not satisfy the first two conditions the game automaton always halts in a rejecting state, since player $0'$ always checks that these conditions are satisfied. Thus let $\sigma'$ be a strategy of player $1'$ which does not satisfy the third condition.

Let $\phi$ be any simulating strategy of $M'$. We define strategy $\psi$ in terms of $\phi$ and $\sigma'$ just as in Claim 5.3.

As in Claim 5.3, $\psi$ is well-defined and is valid. It remains to prove that $v_\psi \geq v_{\sigma'}$. We first derive an expression for $v_\psi - v_{\sigma'}$ in terms of the visible histories in $\mathcal{VH}$. Again, define $prob[VH]$, $accept[\sigma', VH]$ and $accept[\psi, VH]$ as in Claim 5.3. We claim that

$$v_\psi - v_{\sigma'} = \sum_{VH \in \mathcal{VH}} prob[VH]( accept[\psi, VH] - accept[\sigma', VH] ) .$$

The proof is the same as in Claim 5.3, except to show that for any visible history $VH \in \mathcal{VH}$, $accept[\psi, VH] - accept[\sigma', VH] > 0$. Fix some $VH \in \mathcal{VH}$. Suppose the symbol listed by player $1'$ in the transition from $VH$ to $\sigma'(VH)$ is the $k$th symbol of $m_i$ for some $k$ and $i$. If $VH$ has occurred, player $0'$ cannot have decided to check any symbol listed *before* the $k$th symbol of $m_i$. This is because as soon as player $0'$ checks a symbol, it halts, and player $1'$ lists no further symbols. Since player $0'$ has not already decided to check a symbol, the probability that player $0'$ checks the $k$th symbol of $m_i$ is $\frac{7}{8}$. If player $0'$ checks this symbol, it halts in a rejecting state when player $1'$ uses strategy $\sigma'$ because player $1'$ lists an invalid symbol in the transition from $VH$ to $\sigma'(VH)$. This proves that $accept[\sigma', VH] \leq \frac{1}{8}$.

In a similar way, we prove that $\frac{1}{8} < accept[\psi, VH]$. If player $1'$ uses strategy $\psi$, it lists a valid symbol in the transition from $VH$ to $\psi(VH)$. With probability $\frac{7}{8}$ player $0'$ checks that the symbol is valid and if it is, it restarts the algorithm from scratch. Since player $1'$ simulates strategy $\phi$ once the algorithm is restarted, the probability $M$ halts in an accepting state is $\geq \frac{1}{4}$, since we assume that on *any* strategy of player 1 on $x$, player 0 halts in an accepting state with probability $> \frac{1}{4}$. Hence the conditional probability that an accepting state is reached, given visible history $VH$ is $\geq \frac{7}{8}\frac{1}{4} > \frac{1}{8}$ and so $\frac{1}{8} < accept[\psi, VH]$. We have now shown that for any $VH \in \mathcal{VH}$, $accept[\sigma', VH] \leq \frac{1}{8} < accept[\psi, VH]$. Since $prob[VH] \geq 0$ for all $VH \in \mathcal{VH}$, it follows that

$$v_\psi - v_{\sigma'} = \sum_{VH \in \mathcal{VH}} prob[VH]( accept[\psi, VH] - accept[\sigma', VH] ) > 0 .$$

This completes the proof that $v_\psi \geq v_{\sigma'}$, and so the claim is proved. $\square$

# 5.2  History Bounded Game Automata

We mentioned in the introduction that space bounded game automata with partial information are hard to characterize. By definition, in such a game a strategy of player 1 is a function of the whole history of the game visible to player 1. In a game of complete information, we can assume without loss of generality that player 1 always uses a Markov strategy. However such an assumption cannot be made for game automata with partial information. Intuitively, this is so because in a game of complete information, the complete configuration of the game at any step is visible to player 1, and hence at any step the best choice of player 1 can be determined from the configuration at that step. In contrast, at a step of a game of partial information the configuration of the game which is visible to player 1 does not include the private tapes and states of player 0. There may be many possible complete configurations of the game consistent with the configuration visible to player 1. The history of the game determines the relative probability of each possible configuration. The optimal next step of player 1 at any step of the game may depend on the probability distribution of the complete configurations at the beginning of the step and thus on the whole history of the game.

In time bounded game automata with partial information this is not a problem since the history on which a strategy of player 1 can depend is necessarily limited to the running time of the game. However in space bounded game automata there is no limit on the running time; hence the strategy of player 1 can depend on a history of unbounded length. Since in a space bounded game automaton the history is unbounded, the relative probabilities of the possible configurations invisible to player 1 may require an arbitrarily large amount of space to write down.

Since we do not have a characterization of game automata with unlimited history bound, we concentrate instead on game automata with a limited history bound. In Chapter 2 we defined history as a resource of a game automaton as follows. Let $M$ be a probabilistic game automaton. A strategy $\sigma$ on input $x$ of length $n$ has *history* bound $h$ if $\sigma(visible(H_1, 1)) = \sigma(visible(H_2, 1))$ for any pair of histories of $M$ on $x$ such that the sequences of the last $h$ visible configurations of $visible(H_1, 1)$ and $visible(H_2, 1))$ are the same. Intuitively, the strategy $\sigma$ depends only on the last $h$ configurations of the history visible to player 1. Clearly if $\sigma$ is a Markov strategy then $\sigma$ has history bound 1. We say game automaton $M$ with bound $\epsilon$ is $h(n)$ history bounded if for any input of length $n$ accepted by $M$, there is a strategy $\sigma$ of $M$ that has history bound $h(n)$ and is a bounded winning strategy of $M$ on $x$ with bound $\epsilon$, that is, $v_\sigma > \frac{1}{2} + \epsilon$.

We use the notation $G$-$SPACE,HIS(s(n), h(n))$ to denote the class of languages accepted by game automata in the class $G$ with space bound $s(n)$ and history bound $h(n)$. For example, $UP$–$SPACE, HIS(s(n), h(n))$ denotes the class of languages accepted by game automata in the class $UP$ with these bounds. As this notation is a little cumbersome, we shorten it for the special case of Markov game automata to which we will refer often. We denote the class $G$–$SPACE, HIS(s(n), 1)$, where $G$ is any type of game automaton, by $GM$–$SPACE(s(n))$. Our first main result is that space bounded Markov game automata recognize the same languages as nondeterministic Turing machines that run in time exponential in $s(n)$. This is proved in Theorem 5.9; the proof uses the following lemma.

**Lemma 5.8** *Let $s(n)$ be space constructible and let $M$ be a $s(n)$ space bounded game automaton from the class $\forall UM$ (UM, BM or $\forall BM$). Then there is an $s(n)$ space bounded game automaton $M'$ from the class $\forall UM$ (UM, BM or $\forall BM$, respectively) that accepts the same language as $M$, halts with probability 1 and runs in expected time $2^{2^{O(s(n))}}$ on any Markov strategies of the players of $M'$.*

**Proof:** The proof is identical to the proof of a similar result for games of complete information in Lemma 4.5. □

**Theorem 5.9** *For space constructible $s(n) = \Omega(\log n)$,*

$$\cup_c NTIME(2^{cs(n)}) = BM\text{–}SPACE(s(n)) = UM\text{–}SPACE(s(n))$$
$$= \forall BM\text{–}SPACE(s(n)) = \forall UM\text{–}SPACE(s(n)) .$$

**Proof:** We will show that $\forall UM$–$SPACE(s(n)) \subseteq \cup_c NTIME(2^{cs(n)})$ and that $\cup_c NTIME(2^{cs(n)}) \subseteq BM$–$SPACE(s(n))$. The theorem follows immediately from these two facts.

First we show that $\forall UM$–$SPACE(s(n)) \subseteq \cup_c NTIME(2^{cs(n)})$. The proof of this is very similar to the proof of Theorem 4.16. Let $M$ be an $s(n)$ space bounded game automaton in the class $\forall UM$ and let $d^{s(n)}$ be an upper bound on the number of configurations of $M$ on an input of length $n$. From Lemma 5.8, assume without loss of generality that $M$ halts with probability 1 on all inputs. We describe a nondeterministic Turing machine $M'$ that recognizes the same language as $M$ in time $O(d^{s(n)})$. Before we can describe $M'$, we need to show how the graph representation of space bounded game automata of complete information, introduced in Section 4.1, can be modified to space bounded Markov game automata.

Fix an input $x$. In Section 4.1, we described a graph representation of a space bounded game automaton in the class $\forall UC$ on $x$. A graph representation of a game automaton in the class $\forall UM$ on $x$ is defined in exactly the same way. Thus if $G$ is the graph representation of $M$ on $x$, each node of $G$ is labeled by a distinct configuration of $M$ on $x$, and the nodes of $G$ are partitioned into universal, existential, coin-tossing and halting nodes. Let $N = O(d^{s(n)})$ be the number of nodes of $G$. Other than the halting nodes, each node has two outgoing edges. Let $\{1, \ldots, N\}$ be the nodes of $G$. There is an edge from node $i$ to node $j$ in the graph if there is a transition from the configuration labeling node $i$ to the configuration labeling node $j$ in $M$.

Consider a subgraph of $G$ obtained by removing one of the two edges from each existential node and each universal node of $G$. The set of remaining outgoing edges from the existential (universal) nodes of the subgraph is called an *existential policy* $\sigma$ (*universal policy* $\tau$) of $G$. We denote the subgraph as $G_{\sigma,\tau}$. However, unlike graphs representing game automata of complete information, an existential policy $\sigma$ of $G$ may not correspond to a Markov strategy of player 1 of $M$ on $x$. This is because $M$ is a game of partial information and so for any Markov strategy $\sigma$ of $M$, $\sigma(visible(H_1, 1)) = \sigma(visible(H_2, 1))$ if $visible(last(H_1), 1) = visible(last(H_2), 1)$.

We define the set of *valid existential policies* to be a subset of the existential policies of $G$ such that there is a one-to-one correspondence between valid policies of $G$ and Markov strategies of $M$. A policy $\sigma$ is a valid existential policy if it satisfies the following property. Let $(i, j)$ and $(i', j')$ be any pair of edges in policy $\sigma$. Let $C_i, C_{i'}, C_j$ and $C_{j'}$ be the configurations labeling nodes $i, i', j$ and $j'$, respectively. Then $visible(C_i, 1) = visible(C_{i'}, 1) \Rightarrow visible(C_j, 1) = visible(C_{j'}, 1)$. It is straightforward to show that there is a one-to-one correspondence between the valid policies of $G$ and the Markov strategies of $M$.

By the definition of language acceptance of a Markov game, $x$ is accepted by $M$ if and only if there exists a Markov strategy $\sigma$ of player 1 of $M$ on $x$

such that $v_\sigma > \frac{1}{2}$. Let $G$ be the graph representation of $M$ on $x$. From Claim 4.3, $x$ is accepted by $M$ if and only if there exists a valid existential policy $\sigma$ of $G$ such that

$$\min_\tau \{v_{\sigma,\tau}(start(G_{\sigma,\tau}))\} > \frac{1}{2} ,$$

where $G_{\sigma,\tau}$ is the subgraph of $G$ with respect to policies $\sigma$ and $\tau$.

We now describe the nondeterministic Turing machine $M'$ that accepts the same language as $M$. On input $x$, $M'$ constructs the graph $G$ that represents $M$ on input $x$. Then $M'$ existentially chooses an existential policy $\sigma$ of $G$. $M'$ checks that the chosen policy is valid. If not, $M'$ halts in a rejecting state. Finally $M'$ computes

$$\min_\tau \{v_{\sigma,\tau}(start(G_{\sigma,\tau}))\} .$$

If this quantity is $> \frac{1}{2}$ then $M'$ accepts $x$; otherwise $M'$ rejects $x$.

Clearly $M'$ accepts $x$ if and only if $M$ accepts $x$. It remains to show that $M'$ runs in time $2^{O(s(n))}$. We show that on an input of length $n$, $M'$ runs in time polynomial in $N$, the number of nodes in the graph representing $M$ on $x$. Since $N = 2^{O(s(n))}$, this implies that $M$ runs in time $2^{O(s(n))}$.

Since $G$ has $N$ nodes, $M$ requires time at most polynomial in $N$ to construct $G$ and to choose a policy $\sigma$ of $G$. $M'$ can also check in time polynomial in $N$ if the policy chosen is a valid policy, using the definition of a valid policy. We need to show that $\min_\tau \{v_{\sigma,\tau}(start(G_{\sigma,\tau}))\}$ can be computed in time polynomial in $N$. We claim that this is the value $v(start(G))$ where for $1 \le i \le N$, $v(i)$ is the solution to the following linear programming problem: maximize $\sum_{i=1}^{N} v(i)$, subject to the constraints

$v(i) = 0$, if $i = N - 1$,
$v(i) = 1$, if $i = N$,
$v(i) = \frac{1}{2}[v(j) + v(k)]$,
    if $i$ is a cointossing node of $G$ with outgoing edges $(i, j), (i, k)$,
$v(i) \le v(j)$,
    if $i$ is a universal node of $G$ with outgoing edge $(i, j)$,
$v(i) \le v(j)$,
    if $i$ is an existential node of $G$ and $(i, j) \in \sigma$ .

The proof of this is similar to the proof of Lemma 4.13. Since the linear programming problem can be solved in time polynomial in $N$, just as in Theorem 4.13, $M'$ uses time polynomial in $N$. Hence $\forall UM\text{-}SPACE(s(n)) \subseteq \cup_{c \geq 0} NTIME(2^{cs(n)})$, as required.

We next show that $\cup_c NTIME(2^{cs(n)}) \subseteq BM\text{-}SPACE(s(n))$. The proof is similar to the proof that $UC\text{-}SPACE(s(n)) \subseteq UP\text{-}SPACE(s(n))$, given in Theorem 5.1. Let $M$ be a nondeterministic Turing machine with time bound $2^{cs(n)}$ for some $c$. We describe a game $M'$ that recognizes the same language as $M$.

In keeping with the notation in the rest of this thesis, we call a computation of $M$ a history. Intuitively the simulation of $M'$ by $M$ works as follows. Fix some input $x$ of length $n$. Player $1'$ of $M'$ existentially simulates a history of $M$ on $x$ by listing each symbol of the history in sequence. If player $1'$ lists a halting configuration at some step, $M'$ halts in an accepting state if and only if the configuration is accepting. Player $0'$ checks that the sequence of symbols listed by player $1'$ is a valid history of $M$ and halts in a rejecting state if the history is not valid. Since player $0'$ is bounded by $O(\log s(n))$ space, it cannot check the complete history listed by player $1'$. Hence player $0'$ randomly and privately decides whether to check one symbol of the history. After each step where player $1'$ has listed a symbol of the history, player $0'$ checks the symbol with probability $\frac{3}{4}$. The difference between this simulation and the simulation of Theorem 5.1 is that if player $0'$ checks a symbol of the history that is valid, then the simulation starts from scratch again. Just as in the simulation of Theorem 5.1, if the symbol is invalid, player $0'$ halts in a rejecting state. With probability $\frac{1}{4}$ player $0'$ does not check the symbol and player 1 lists the next symbol of the history. Since player $1'$ does not know when player $0'$ is checking the listing, it is forced to output a valid history.

Player $1'$ lists a history of $M$ just as in Theorem 5.1, as a string of the form $m_0 a_1 m_1 \ldots a_i m_i \ldots$, where each $m_i$ is a configuration, $m_0$ is the initial configuration and $m_{i-1} \overset{a_i}{\to} m_i$ for $i > 0$, that is, the $a_i th$ possible next configuration from $m_{i-1}$ is $m_i$, according to the transition function of $M$. In this simulation, unlike the simulation of Theorem 5.1, player $1'$ maintains two counters on its worktape; one to count how many configurations of $M$ it has listed so far, and the other to count how many symbols of the current configuration have already been listed. The reason for this will become clear when we argue that on inputs accepted by $M$, player $1'$ has a bounded winning Markov strategy.

Note that since the running time of $M$ is bounded by $2^{O(s(n))}$, the length of these counters is $O(s(n))$.

The way that player $0'$ checks that the history listed by player $1'$ is valid is also just as in Theorem 5.1. It is made simpler by the fact that player $1'$ never lists a coin-tossing move, since $M$ has no randomness. The checking algorithm is described in Figure 5.2. To summarize, the main difference between the simulation of this theorem and the simulation of Theorem 5.1 is that player $1'$ maintains two extra counters, one to count how many configurations of $M$ it has listed so far, and the other to count how many symbols of the current configuration have already been listed.

> **procedure** *generalcheck*;
>     if **not** *checking* then
>         with probability $\frac{3}{4}$ *checking* := true; *checkcount* := 0;
>
>     if *checking* then
>         *checkcount* := *checkcount* +1;
>         if *checkcount* $\in \{1, \ldots, 4\}$   then record *symbol*;
>         if $k = s(n) + 1$         then record *symbol* $a_i$;
>         if *checkcount* $= s(n) + 1$   then check *symbol* is valid;
>             if not valid then reject
>         else
>             /* restart simulation */
>             /* set all variables to initial values */
>             *oddconfiguration* := false;
>             *checking* := false;
>             $k := 0$;
>             *initial* := true;
>             move all tape heads to inital position

Figure 5.4: *General checking procedure, Theorem 5.8.*

It is straightforward to check that $M'$ uses space $O(s(n))$. Before showing that $M$ and $M'$ accept the same language, we review some notation which was introduced in Theorem 5.1. Fix an arbitrary input $x$. Let $\sigma'$ be any strategy of player $1'$ on $x$. If the string listed by player $1'$ on strategy $\sigma'$ on *any* sequence of coin tosses of player $0'$ is valid, we say $\sigma'$ is a *valid* strategy. Otherwise $\sigma'$ is an *invalid* strategy.

Also as in Theorem 5.1, we call a history of $M'$ where player $0'$ checks a symbol a *checking history*. A history of $M'$ where player $0'$ does not check a symbol is called a *non-checking history*. Each path of a computation tree $T_{\sigma'}$ is labeled by a history. If the history is a checking history, then the corresponding path in the computation tree is called a checking path; otherwise the path is called a non-checking path. Each non-checking path of $T_{\sigma'}$ is a simulation of some history of $M$; there is a one-to-one correspondence between the non-checking paths of $T_{\sigma'}$ and the paths of $T_{\sigma}$.

The proof that $M'$ and $M$ accept the same language is divided into the following three claims.

**Claim 5.10** *Let $M$ and $M'$ be defined as above. If $x$ is accepted by $M$ then for some Markov strategy of player $1'$ of $M'$, $v_{\sigma'} = 1$.*

**Claim 5.11** *Let $M$ and $M'$ be defined as above and let $\sigma'$ be a valid strategy of $M'$. Then if $x$ is not accepted by $M$, $v_{\sigma'} = 0$.*

**Claim 5.12** *Let $M$ and $M'$ be defined as above and let $\sigma'$ be an invalid strategy of $M'$ on $x$. Then $v_{\sigma'} \leq \frac{1}{4}$.*

Before proving these claims, we show how they can be combined to prove that $M'$ and $M$ accept the same langauge, where $M'$ has bound $\frac{1}{4}$. Suppose $M$ accepts $x$. Then some Markov strategy $\sigma'$ of $M'$ on $x$ has value 1 by Claim 5.10. Hence player $1'$ has a Markov bounded winning strategy on input $x$ and so $x$ is accepted by $M'$. Otherwise $M$ does not accept $x$. Then from Claim 5.11, for all valid strategies $\sigma'$ of $M'$, $v_{\sigma'} = 0$. Thus all valid strategies $\sigma'$ of player $1'$ must be bounded losing strategies. Furthermore by Claim 5.12, all invalid strategies of $M'$ must also be bounded losing strategies and so $x$ is rejected by $M'$. Hence $M'$ is a bounded random Markov game automaton and $M'$ accepts the same language as $M$. We now turn to the proofs of the claims.

**Proof of Claim 5.10:** If $x$ is accepted by $M$ then there exists a history of $M$ on $x$ for which $last(H)$ is an accepting configuration. Fix some such history

$H$. We claim that a Markov winning strategy of player $1'$ is to list the history $H$ of $M$ on $x$. Any symbol of the history $H$ of $M$ is fully determined by the number of its configuration and its position within that configuration. Since player $1'$ keeps these counters on its worktape, the symbol it lists at every step is fully determined by the contents of its worktape. Hence this strategy is a Markov strategy of player $1'$. Next we show that it is a winning strategy.

Let $p_{check}$ be the probability that player $0'$ checks a symbol listed by player $1'$, that is, $p_{check}$ is the probability of following a checking path of $T_{\sigma'}$. If player $0'$ does not check a symbol listed by player $1'$, player $1'$ eventually lists an accepting configuration, namely $last(H)$ and player $0'$ halts in an accepting state. Thus the probability of reaching an accepting leaf on a non-checking path of $T_{\sigma'}$ is 1. If a checking path is followed then since the simulation is restarted, the probability of reaching an accepting leaf is $v_{\sigma'}$. Thus $v_{\sigma'}$ satisfies $v_{\sigma'} = p_{check}v_{\sigma'} + (1 - p_{check})1$. Hence $v_{\sigma'} = 1$. $\square$

**Proof of Claim 5.11:** The proof of this claim is similar to the proof of Claim 5.10. If $x$ is not accepted by $M$ then for all histories of $M$ on $x$, $last(H)$ is a rejecting configuration. Let $\sigma'$ be any valid strategy of player $1'$. Let $p_{check}$ be the probability that player $0'$ checks a symbol listed by player $1'$, that is, $p_{check}$ is the probability of following a checking path of $T_{\sigma'}$. If player $0'$ does not check a symbol listed by player $1'$, player $1'$ eventually lists a rejecting configuration and player $0'$ halts in a rejecting state. Thus the probability of reaching an accepting leaf on a non-checking path of $T_{\sigma'}$ is 0. If a checking path is followed then since the simulation is restarted, the probability of reaching an accepting leaf is $v_{\sigma'}$. Thus $v_{\sigma'}$ satisfies $v_{\sigma'} = p_{check}v_{\sigma'} + (1 - p_{check})0$ and so $v_{\sigma'} = 0$. $\square$

**Proof of Claim 5.12:** The proof of this claim is similar to the proof of Claim 5.3. Let $\mathcal{VH}$ be the set of valid visible histories $VH$ such that in the transition from $VH$ to $\sigma'(VH)$, player $1'$ lists an invalid symbol. We first derive an expression for $v_{\sigma'}$ in terms of the visible histories in $\mathcal{VH}$. For $VH \in \mathcal{VH}$, let $prob[VH]$ be the probability of following a path of $T_{\sigma'}$ which is labeled by a history with visible prefix $VH$. Let $accept[\sigma', VH]$ denote the conditional probability of reaching an accepting leaf of $T_{\sigma'}$, given that a path is followed which is labeled by a history with visible prefix $VH$. We claim that

$$v_{\sigma'} = \sum_{VH \in \mathcal{VH}} prob[VH]accept[\sigma', VH] .$$

To see this, first note that any valid path of $T_{\sigma'}$ must end in a rejecting leaf since for every history $H$ of $M$ on $x$, $last(H)$ is a rejecting configuration. Since the probabilities $prob[VH]$ and $prob[VH']$ are independent for distinct $VH$, $VH' \in \mathcal{VH}$, the value $v_{\sigma'}$ equals the sum over all $VH \in \mathcal{VH}$ of $prob[VH]accept[\sigma', VH]$. Finally we show that $accept[\sigma', VH] < \frac{1}{4}$ for any visible history $VH \in \mathcal{VH}$. Fix some $VH \in \mathcal{VH}$. Suppose the symbol listed by player $1'$ in the transition from $VH$ to $\sigma'(VH)$ is the $kth$ symbol of $m_i$ for some $k$ and $i$. If $VH$ has occurred, player $0'$ cannot have decided to check any symbol listed *before* the $kth$ symbol of $m_i$. This is because as soon as player $0'$ checks a symbol, it halts, and player $1'$ lists no further symbols. Since player $0'$ has not already decided to check a symbol, the probability that player $0'$ checks the $kth$ symbol of $m_i$ is $\frac{3}{4}$. If player $0'$ checks this symbol, it halts in a rejecting state when player $1'$ uses strategy $\sigma'$ because player $1'$ lists an invalid symbol in the transition from $VH$ to $\sigma'(VH)$. This proves that $accept[\sigma', VH] \leq \frac{1}{4}$. Hence

$$
\begin{aligned}
v_{\sigma'} &= \sum_{VH \in \mathcal{VH}} prob[VH]accept[\sigma', VH] \\
&\leq \frac{1}{4} \sum_{VH \in \mathcal{VH}} prob[VH] \\
&< \frac{1}{4} \ .
\end{aligned}
$$

This completes the proof that $v_{\sigma'} < \frac{1}{4}$, and so the claim is proved. $\square$

To complete this section, we show that the history bound of a game can be decreased at the cost of increasing the space.

**Theorem 5.13** *If $h(n)$ is space constructible,*

$$
UP\text{--}SPACE, HIS(s(n), h(n)) \subseteq UM\text{--}SPACE(s(n) + h(n)) \ .
$$

**Proof:** Let $M$ be a game automaton in the class $UP$ with space and history bounds $s(n)$ and $h(n)$, respectively. We describe a game automaton $M'$ that simulates $M$. Fix an input $x$ of length $n$. Player $0'$ of $M'$ simulates the steps of player $0$ of $M$ and player $1'$ of $M'$ simulates the steps of player $1$ of $M$. Also, player $1'$ records on a tape some extra information that uniquely defines the last $h(n)$ visible configurations of $M$ which it has simulated. After visible step $k$ of the simulation, if $k < h(n)$, the extra information consists of the initial visible configuration of the game and a sequence of numbers $\alpha_1 \ldots \alpha_k$. Otherwise when $k \geq h(n)$, the extra information consists of the visible configuration, other than the input, at step $k - h(n) + 1$ and a sequence of numbers $\alpha_{k-h(n)+2} \ldots \alpha_k$. We describe these numbers in more detail in the next paragraph. Since $h(n)$ is space constructible, player $1'$ can test whether $k \leq h(n)$ or whether $k > h(n)$.

The sequence of numbers that player $1'$ records is similar to the sequence in Theorem 3.5. Given visible configuration of $M$ at time $k$, there is at most a constant number, $a$ of possible visible configurations of $M$ at time $k+1$. This is because in changing the visible configuration in one step, a player of $M$ can only change the visible state, the visible tape head positions and the contents of a constant number of tape cells. The $a$ possible visible configurations can be ordered in a straightforward way so that any number $\alpha$, $1 \leq \alpha \leq a$, uniquely determines the $\alpha th$ possible next configuration from any given configuration.

In general we denote the $ith$ visible configuration of $M$ that is simulated by the players of $M'$ by $VC_i$ and the initial configuration is $VC_0$. Before the $kth$ visible step of the simulation, the tapes of player $1'$ contain a visible configuration that is $VC_0$ if $k < h(n)$ and is denoted by $VC_{k-h(n)}$ otherwise. Also the tapes of player $1'$ contain a sequence $\alpha_{k-h(n)+1} \ldots \alpha_{k-1}$. The current visible configuration of the simulation, $VC_{k-1}$, is also visible to player $1'$. After the $kth$ visible step of the simulation, player $1'$ records on a tape the $\alpha_k$ whichx determines the visible step just taken. If $k \geq h(n)$, player $1'$ computes the visible configuration $VC_{k-h(n)+1}$ such that $VC_{k-h(n)} \overset{\alpha_{k-h(n)+1}}{\rightarrow} VC_{k-h(n)+1}$. Then player $1'$ erases the number $\alpha_{k-h(n)+1}$, so that exactly $h(n)$ numbers $\alpha_i$ are recorded on the tape. Player $1'$ also erases $VC_{k-h(n)}$. Thus after the $kth$ visible step, the tapes of player $1'$ contain

$$VC_{k-i+1}\alpha_{k-i+2} \ldots \alpha_k VC_k \ ,$$

where $i = h(n)$ if $k \geq h(n)$ and $i = k+1$ otherwise. The sequence $\alpha_{k-i+2} \ldots \alpha_k$ represents the visible configurations $VC_{k-i+2} \ldots VC_k$ of $M$ where for $k-i+1 \leq j \leq k$, $VC_{j-1} \overset{\alpha_j}{\rightarrow} VC_j$.

We need to show that $M'$ accepts the same language as $M$ and that $M'$ is a Markov game automaton. To see this, fix an arbitrary input $x$ of length $n$. Let $\sigma'$ be a Markov strategy of player $1'$ of $M'$. We say $\sigma'$ *simulates* strategy $\sigma$ of $M$ on $x$ if for any history $H'$ of $M'$ with $visible(last(H'), 1) = VC_{k-i}\alpha_{k-i+1} \ldots \alpha_{k-1} VC_{k-1}$, and

$$\sigma'(visible(H', 1)) = VC_{k-i+1}\alpha_{k-i+2} \ldots \alpha_{k-1}\sigma(visible(H, 1)),$$

where $H$ is any history of $M$ such that $VC_{k-i}, \ldots VC_{k-1}$ are the last $i$ visible configurations of $visible(H, 1)$.

It is straightforward to show that every strategy $\sigma'$ of player $1'$ simulates some strategy $\sigma$ of player 1. Also if $\sigma'$ simulates strategy $\sigma$ then $v_{\sigma'} = v_\sigma$. Hence if $M$ accepts $x$, some strategy of $M$ with history bound $h(n)$ is a winning strategy of player 1 of $M$ on $x$ and thus some Markov strategy of player $1'$ is a winning strategy on $x$. On the other hand, if $M$ does not accept $x$ then no strategy of player $1'$ on $x$ is a winning strategy. Thus $M'$ and $M$ accept the same language. $\square$

# 6

## Conclusion

We have defined a new general model of a computational game, called a probabilistic game automaton. We have shown that this model provides a uniform framework for the study of game-like phenomena in a computational setting. We have given a precise description of the probabilistic game automaton, and have shown how it includes as special cases the Arthur-Merlin games of Babai [2], the interactive proof systems of Goldwasser, Micali and Rackoff [19], and other game classes studied in the computer science literature [25], [27], [30]. Also, the model includes other complexity classes of games not previously studied, such as the games against unknown nature of Chapter 3 and the space bounded game automata of Chapters 4 and 5. Finally, we have related a number of the complexity classes of games encompassed by the model to each other and to standard computational complexity classes.

There still remain many open problems on the complexity of game automata. First, there is room for improvement on some of the results of this thesis. For example in the simulation of Theorem 3.5 we eliminate partial information from unbounded random game automata without universal moves at the cost of squaring the running time. Is there a way to simulate an unbounded random game automaton with partial information by one with complete information, without squaring the running time? A related problem is whether polynomial time bounded game automata in the class $\forall UP$ can be simulated by polynomial time alternating Turing machines.

Another problem which has not been resolved is the complexity of the class of languages accepted by space bounded game automata with partial information. We have shown that such game automata are more powerful than game automata with complete information (Theorems 5.4 and 5.1) but do not have a good characterization of these classes. For example, is $UP\text{--}SPACE(\log(s(n))) \subseteq UC\text{--}SPACE(s(n))$? A subclass of space bounded game automata of partial information which may be more tractable is the class that always halts on every input. Can tight results on the complexity of this subclass be obtained?

A related question is to characterize the class $\forall UC\text{--}SPACE(s(n))$, which is the class of languages accepted by space bounded game automata of complete information with coin-tossing, existential and universal moves. We have shown $\forall UC\text{--}SPACE(s(n)) \subseteq \cup_c NTIME(2^{cs(n)})$ but conjecture that the containment is proper.

A resource which we have not examined in this thesis is the number of alternations, or moves of the players. For example, game automata with constant number of alternations between the players are an interesting subclass of the general game classes. We mentioned in Chapter 3 that Babai [2] proved that polynomially time bounded Arthur-Merlin games with a constant number of alternations between the players can be simulated by Arthur-Merlin games with just one alternation, that is, a game with two moves, the first move being Arthur's. A question posed by Babai is whether $BC\text{--}TIME(poly(n)) \subseteq \Sigma_k^P$, where $poly(n)$ is any polynomial function of $n$ and $\Sigma_k^P$ is the class of polynomial time bounded alternating Turing machines with $k$ alternations, starting with the existential player. Similar questions remain unsolved for other game models.

There are a number of ways that the model introduced here could be extended to include other features of games. First, the restriction that player 1 displays complete information could be removed. It would be interesting to see if the results of the thesis extend to this general model. Another way to extend the model is to increase the number of players. An analysis of games with more than two players would be complicated by the fact that in a multi-person game, subgroups of the players may form coalitions. However such games may model more accurately the game-like features of a distributed system. Cooperation between the players is another feature of games which is missing from our model. A third way to generalize the model of games defined in this thesis is to have payoffs for the players at the end of a game, which depend on the outcome of the game. In a probabilistic game automaton, there are only two outcomes — accept or reject. This could be generalized to allow integer payoffs for the players. Finally, it would be interesting to explore applications of these models to problems in cryptography and distributed computing.

# Bibliography

[1] W. AIELLO, S. GOLDWASSER, and J. HASTAD. On the power of interaction. In *Proceedings of the 27th IEEE Symposium on the Foundations of Computer Science*, pages 368–379, October 1986.

[2] L. BABAI. Trading group theory for randomness. In *Proceedings of the Seventeenth ACM Symposium Theory of Computing*, pages 421–429, May 1985.

[3] R. W. BALL and R. A. BEAUMONT. *Introduction to Modern Algebra and Matrix Theory*. Reinhart and Company, Inc., New York, 1956.

[4] M. BEN-OR, S. GOLDWASSER, J. KILLIAN, and A. WIGDERSON. Multi-prover interactive proofs: How to remove intractibility. In *Proceedings of the Twentieth ACM Symposium on the Theory of Computing*, pages 113–131, May 1988.

[5] M. BEN-OR and N. LINIAL. Collective coin flipping, robust voting schemes and minima of Banzhaf values. In *Proceedings of the 26th IEEE Symposium on the Foundations of Computer Science*, pages 408–416, October 1985.

[6] L. BERMAN. The complexity of logical theories. *Theoretical Computer Science*, 11:71–77, 1980.

[7] M. BLUM and S. KANNAN. Designing programs that check their work. In *Proceedings of the Twenty-First ACM Symposium on the Theory of Computing*, May 1989.

[8] G. BRASSARD and C. CREPEAU. Nontransitive transfer of confidence: a perfect zero knowledge protocol for SAT and beyond. In *Proceedings of the 27th IEEE Symposium on the Foundations of Computer Science*, pages 188–195, October 1986.

[9] A. K. CHANDRA, D.C. KOZEN, and L.J. STOCKMEYER. Alternation. *Journal of the Association of Computing Machinery*, 28(1):114–133, 1981.

[10] A. CONDON and R. J. LIPTON. Upper bounds on the complexity of space bounded interactive proof systems. Technical Report 841, University of Wisconsin-Madison, 1989.

[11] S. A. COOK. A taxonomy of problems with fast parallel algorithms. *Information and Control*, 64:2–22, January 1985.

[12] C. DERMAN. *Finite State Markov Decision Processes*. Academic Press, 1972.

[13] C. DWORK and L. STOCKMEYER. Interactive proof systems with finite state verifiers. Research Report RJ 6262 (61659), IBM Almaden Research Center, San Jose, CA, 1988.

[14] U. FEIGE and A. SHAMIR. Multi-oracle interactive protocols with space bounded verifiers. In *Proceedings of the Conference on Structure in Complexity Theory*, June 1989.

[15] L. FORTNOW, J. ROMPEL, and M. SIPSER. On the power of multi-prover interactive protocols. In *Proceedings of the Conference on Structure in Complexity Theory*, pages 156–161, June 1988.

[16] M.R. GAREY and D.S. JOHNSON. *Computers and Intractibility: A guide to the theory of NP-Completeness*. W.H. Freeman and Company, 1979.

[17] J. GILL. The computational complexity of probabilistic turing machines. *SIAM Journal on Computing*, 6:675–695, 1977.

[18] O. GOLDREICH, S. MICALI, and A. WIGDERSON. Proofs that yield nothing but their validity and a methodology of cryptographic design. In *Proceedings of the 27th IEEE Symposium on the Foundations of Computer Science*, pages 174–187, October 1986.

[19] S. GOLDWASSER, S. MICALI, and C. RACKOFF. The knowledge complexity of interactive protocols. In *Proceedings of the Seventeenth ACM Symposium Theory of Computing*, pages 291–304, May 1985.

[20] S. GOLDWASSER and M. SIPSER. Private coins versus public coins in interactive proof systems. In *Proceedings of the Eighteenth ACM Symposium Theory of Computing*, pages 59–68, May 1986.

[21] HOWARD. *Dynamic Programming and Markov Processes*. M.I.T. Press, 1960.

[22] D. S. JOHNSON. The NP-completeness column: An ongoing guide. *Journal of Algorithms*, pages 397–411, December 1983.

[23] J.G. KEMENY and J. LAURIE SNELL. *Finite Markov Chains*. D. Van Nostrand Company, Inc., 1960.

[24] L.G. KHACHIYAN. A polynomial algorithm in linear programming. *Soviet Math Dokl.*, 20:191–194, 1979.

[25] R.E. LADNER and J.K. NORMAN. Solitaire automata. *Journal on Computers and System Sciences*, 30(1):116–129, 1985.

[26] R. J. LIPTON. Recursively enumerable languages have finite state interactive proofs. Technical Report CS-TR-213-89, Princeton University, 1989.

[27] C. H. PAPADIMITRIOU. Games against nature. In *Proceedings of the 24th IEEE Symposium on the Foundations of Computer Science*, pages 446–450, 1983.

[28] G.L. PETERSON and J.H. REIF. Multiple person alternation. In *Proceedings of the 20th IEEE Symposium on the Foundations of Computer Science*, pages 348–363, 1979.

[29] M. O. RABIN. A probabilistic algorithm for testing primality. *Journal of Number Theory*, 2:128–138, 1980.

[30] J.H. REIF. The complexity of two-player games of incomplete information. *Journal on Computers and System Sciences*, 29(2):274–301, 1984.

[31] W.L. RUZZO, J. SIMON, and M. TOMPA. Space-bounded hierarchies and probabilistic computations. *Journal on Computers and System Sciences*, 28(2):216–230, April 1984.

[32] C. YAP. Valuation machines. Manuscript from New York University.

# Index

*The MIT Press, with Peter Denning, general consulting editor, and Brian Randall, European consulting editor, publishes computer science books in the following series:*

**ACM Doctoral Dissertation Award and Distinguished Dissertation Series**

**Artificial Intelligence**, Patrick Henry Winston and J. Michael Brady founding editors; J. Michael Brady, Daniel G. Bobrow, and Randall Davis, current editors

**Charles Babbage Institute Reprint Series for the History of Computing**, Martin Campbell-Kelly, editor

**Computer Systems**, Herb Schwetman, editor

**Exploring with Logo**, E. Paul Goldenberg, editor

**Foundations of Computing**, Michael Garey and Albert Meyer, editors

**History of Computing**, I. Bernard Cohen and William Aspray, editors

**Information Systems**, Michael Lesk, editor

**Logic Programming**, Ehud Shapiro, editor; Fernando Pereira, Koichi Furukawa, and D. H. D. Warren, associate editors

**The MIT Electrical Engineering and Computer Science Series**

**Research Monographs in Parallel and Distributed Processing**, Christopher Jesshope and David Klappholz, editors

**Scientific Computation**, Dennis Gannon, editor

**Technical Communication**, Edward Barrett, editor